FRONT COVER: Lost Lands Collections
Model: Jackie Wyers
Hair & Makeup Jackie Wyers
Corset: @french.meadows
BACK COVER: Lost Lands Collections
Model: Jackie Wyers

No part of this magazine may be used, distributed, transmitted or reproduced without the editor's permission.

Contact: imaginarium.magazine.13@gmail.com
Editor: Anastasia Diakidi

Editor & Designer: Anastasia Diakidi
Publisher: KDP / Self-published

Article Photos are public domain unless stated otherwise.
All artists and photographers' photos used with creator's permission.

Contributors:

Evangelia Papanikou
Marcia-Gayscone Masino
Japneet Chandoak
Anastasia Diakidi
Helen Bakopoloulou
Yiannis Kokkinos

CONTENTS

Imaginarium

FEATURES

Editorial	03
Herb Witchery: Lavender	04
Lavender in Magick	08
Bach Remedies	10
Myth: The Apples of Idun	12
Poets Corner	16
Wheel of the Year: Celebrating Ostara	18
Wellbeing: Flower Power in your May Day Bouquet	24
Our friends the Trees	27

Meeting Andrea Gagiu: Thyme to Slice & Dice	30
Recipes by Andreea Gagiu	33
Sabbath: Beltane & Walpurgis Night	36
Elemental Magic: Fire	40
Mythology: Spring is when Moly Blooms	44
Photography: Lost Lands Collections	48

ASTROLOGY

The Witch's Cabinet	54
Planetarium	60
Astrology Lesson: Cusps & House Overlay Pt2	64
Carl Jung & Astrology	70
Aquarius: The Dictatorship of Good Intentions	74
Victorian Floramancy	76

TAROT & DIVINATION

The Fool's Journey: The Visconti–Sforza Deck	80
The Minor Arcana: The Wands	84

ANCIENT WISDOM

Ancient Wisdom	89

Imaginarium | 02

All rights reserved
Photo by Lost Lands Collections
Model: Janice Hampton
Wings: Moon Moth wings by Anne Rea
Corset: French Meadows Corsets

Anastasia Diakidi was born and raised in Rhodes, Greece. She studied Archaeometry and History in the Department of Mediterranean Studies at the University of the Aegean and after graduation continued her studies with Gothic Literature courses at the Phoenix Rising Academy in London, and Mysticism courses at the University of Kent. She continued with Travel Writing seminars at the University of Cambridge. Her love for astrology started at home and very early. In 2018 she started studying astrology at the "Astropaedia" in Athens and she completed her studies in 2020. She also completed her training in traditional Horary astrology with Vasilios Takos in Deborah Houlding's STA (School of Traditional Astrology). In the meantime, she attends courses, seminars and lectures by international astrologers.
She is a member of ISAR. She has been living and working in Canterbury, Kent, UK since 2012.

For astrology lessons and readings contact anastacia.d86@gmail.com or book through the website https://imaginariumworld.co.uk

Dear friends of Imaginarium,

We are now officially in the most beautiful season of the year, spring. Although our lives certainly do not have the bloom of nature, especially in recent years with the events on the world stage that overwhelm us, yet in the world of Imaginarium we always find the magic of life and a way to celebrate it.

In this issue, we once again feature exceptional artists and creators whose work brings beauty not only to our magazine but also to our lives. It is very important to support artists and that is exactly why I created this magazine, where I promote and collaborate with exceptional artists who create that magic that is missing from our lives. Imaginarium Magazine would not be the same without these artists just as our lives would not be the same without the magic that art and by extension those people who provide it.

Thank you so much for supporting the magazine because through your support we are all saying that life is beautiful; it has art, grace, mystery, imagination, and magic.

In this issue, I welcome Marianne Bell, the face behind Lost Lands Collections, who takes us to an ethereal and magical place through her photography. Special thanks to her for the photographic material and the beautiful interview.

I also welcome Andreea Gagiu from Thyme to Slice and Dice. Andreea gives us lovely recipes for spring and together we talk about her love of cooking. I fell in love with her gorgeous desserts and I hope you like them and try making them.

Otherwise, we have a plethora of articles about spring. We talk about the beauty of flowers, the love we get from nature, and how we can use flowers, trees, and nature in general to achieve our well-being.

Thanks once again to our regular contributor Evangelia Papanikou for writing an article about the flower moly, that rare and magical flower that only the gods could cut!

Thanks also to Marcia Gayscone-Masino who wrote for us another beautiful article, this time about Victorian Floramancy! Extremely interesting, I hope you like it.

Finally, I want to greet and welcome to our team, Yannis Kokkinos who has written two articles for this issue. The first one talks about Carl Jung and his contribution to astrology, and the second one is more of a philosophical one, within an astrological context of course, and talks about the Dictatorship of Good Intentions.

I hope you have a beautiful spring, that you enjoy and celebrate with abundance, joy, and magic the two sabbaths of spring, Ostara - aka Easter - and Beltane, and I hope that this solar eclipse that awaits us closes the cycle of sadness to open a new beautiful cycle of joy, love and spring abundance in your life.

Thank you for everything.

Love,
Anastasia Diakidi

Herb Witchery

LAVENDER
LAVANDULA ANGUSTIFOLIA

LAVENDER IN HISTORY & TRADITION

Lavender symbolizes stability and silence. Its name comes from the Latin verb lavare, which means 'to wash'. Indeed, since ancient Greek and Roman times until today, lavender with its distinctive aroma has been around in our bathrooms, laundry, even bedrooms. It blooms from April to August, while its tops must be collected when it is in bloom so that when it dries, its scent remains as well as its beneficial effect.

In ancient times, lavender was being used as an insect repellent when in the countryside or the gardens. In folklore, lovers exchanged lavender flowers as a symbol of devotion. They also said that if a young woman had a pouch of dried lavender on her, she would find her soulmate. In Ireland, tradition has it that if the bride put a sprig of lavender in her garter - which she had to cut from an unmarried woman's garden - she would have a good marriage.

In Egypt, it was quite common to place lavender vessels in the tombs. A three-thousand-year-old vessel was found in the tomb of Tutankhamun, still holding its strong aroma. Lavender was cultivated by the ancient Egyptians in the sacred gardens of Thebes and was used in the ritual of mummification, while they also prepared a cologne to perfume the dead.

In ancient Greece, the sacrificed virgins were adorned with lavender flowers and the prostitutes used lavender to have a cool and fragrant breath.

In ancient Rome, women hid lavender flowers in the carvings of the beds to repel insects but also to awaken their beloved's lust.

Folk tradition has it that Virgin Mary washed the wounds of Jesus with scented lavender water.

Lavender was one of the most popular plants for flower beds and gardens in Britain, both during the Tudor period and in Elizabethan times. The fashion of the time even dictated lavender lawns instead of the classic lawn. In the 17th century, Moira Castle in Ireland gained great fame, thanks to its lavender gardens reaching up to 4 acres. It is believed that St. Hildegard of the Roman Catholic Church, a Benedictine nun, cultivated lavender in her garden in the 12th century and she is credited with the first making of lavender cologne.

For centuries, people spread lavender on the floors, to repel insects; hung cotton bags in the rooms with clothing scraps dipped in its essential oil to repel flies; and often, hung bouquets on the outer walls of houses so the scent of lavender would mask the unpleasant smell of the streets.

In English, there is an obsolete phrase "lay (something) up in lavender", which means I preserve something carefully and place it into storage for future use. The phrase is derived from the old days when in the pawnshop they used to put lavender on the clothes they kept as a pawn.

Imaginarium |04

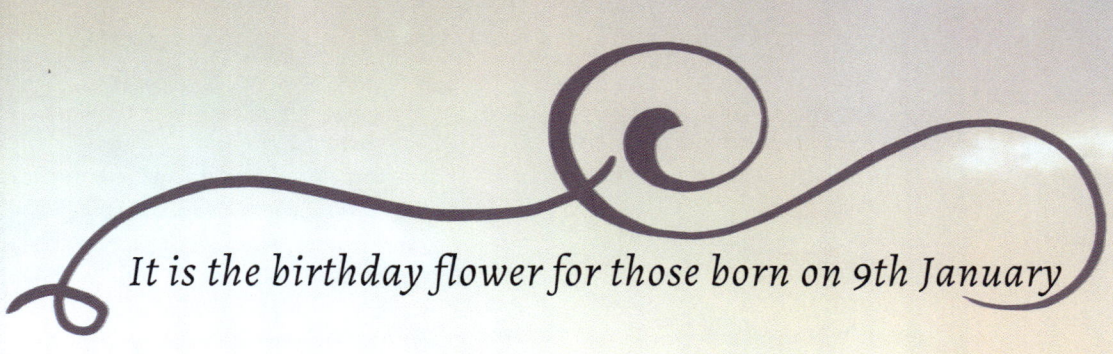

It is the birthday flower for those born on 9th January

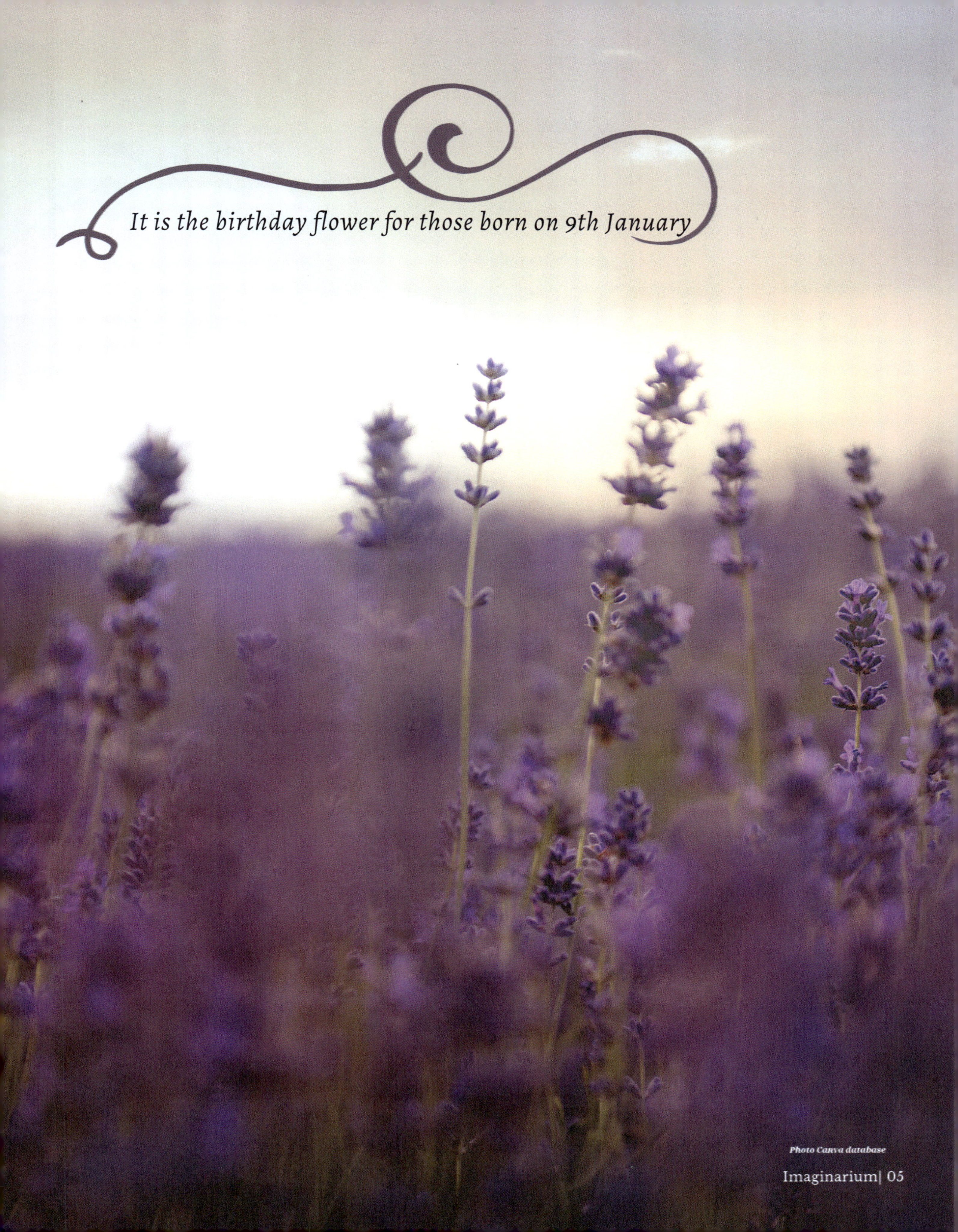

Photo Canva database

Lavender in Aromatherapy & folk medicine

In aromatherapy, it is considered the best essential oil and number one choice in the emergency kit we have at home as lavender's many beneficial properties cover a very wide range of emergencies that we are called to treat ourselves at home. In addition to the body, lavender is an excellent healer of the soul, as it assists in situations such as phobias, hysteria, negative thoughts, nerves, paranoia, panic attacks, anxiety, and much more. There is the so-called phrase of the healers: "if you do not know which herb to use, use lavender".

Of course, we strongly recommend using the herb with medical guidance and, of course, not to be replaced by medical treatment.

Lavender has been used in folk medicine for a long time as a treatment for: depression, fatigue, and joint pains. It was often used as a headache medicine and, rumour has it that Queen Elizabeth I herself, who suffered from migraines, used to drink up to 10 cups of lavender a day to calm her sensitive nerves. Furthermore, people often gargled lavender cologne for toothache… and even treated the sore throat with it, while with the lavender tea, they calmed the tremor and heart diseases.

The 19th-century damsels in distress used to always carry lavender in their handbag to deal with possible fainting. In general, there was so much faith in the healing properties of the herb that it had gained a reputation for offering immunity during the epidemic periods. It is reported that, in the city of Grasse in France, the gloves were perfumed with lavender essential oil; therefore those who made their gloves in that city, never contracted the plague.
However, it is a fact that the essential oil of the plant has excellent antiseptic properties, which helps in the treatment of chronic skin diseases, while it is also a fact that during the First World War lavender was a great assistant in wound disinfection.

In aromatherapy and folk medicine, lavender's uses are numerous: **it is antispasmodic, nerve tonic, stimulant, antimicrobial, antiseptic, antidepressant, antioxidant, sedative, digestive, and treats infections that cause diarrhoea and vomiting. It is also often used in baths to speed up the healing process after childbirth.**
Great also for **tissue reconstruction. Reduces the formation of scars on the skin after cutting, and its oil helps with burns, wounds, abrasions, and bites. It is excellent for many skin problems such as eczema, acne.** It is distinguished for its bactericidal action, and its decoction **tightens the gums and lowers the pressure**. It is an **antidote to snake bites**, and it is said that the hunters in the Alps, when their dog is bitten by a snake, rub lavender on the wound to neutralize the venom. It also **regulates the heart rate and helps the hoarse throat.**

To calm your body and mind when you lie down, have lavender on your pillow and lavender pouches next to your bed. In the room, if there is a lot of intensity, burn lavender essential oil for an hour before going to bed. Also, the decoction of lavender flowers helps in sleep.

In Anthony Askham's Herbal, 1525, it is stated: "For those who do not sleep, put lavender in water and let them take a foot bath at bedtime and put the herb in their temples and they will sleep well by the grace of God"

William Turner, A New Herbal Parts II and III, 1551: "I judge that the flowers of lavender as a decoction and on us, are good in all diseases of the head that come from the common cold and that they effectively rest the mind".

Magick Tips

Put lavender under your pillow while thinking about your wish. Do this before retiring to bed. In the morning, if you have dreamed of something related to your wish, then it will come true. But if you did not have dreams or your dreams were not related to the wish, then it will not come true.

If you dream of a lavender scent in a bottle, you will soon feel disappointed. If you wear clothes in the colour of lavender, pleasant love adventures are on the way. If you dream that you are in a place that smells strongly of lavender and you feel good, then very soon you will have a love affair; while if a woman dreams that she bends down and smells lavender, she will enjoy a fascinating love.

Put some twigs in your closets or pouches with lavender in the pockets of the clothes to fragrance your clothes and protect them from the moth; while if you want to give your furniture a scent, sprinkle the duster with lavender essential oil. Also, a bag of dried lavender in the mop bucket will disinfect the floor, repel insects, and give a wonderful scent to the house.

Love lavender cookies
100gr milk butter
5 grams of powdered sugar
150 grams of all-purpose flour
2 teaspoons dried lavender buds.

Beat the ingredients in the mixer until fluffy. Slowly add the sifted flour and two teaspoons of dried lavender. Roll a thick pastry and with a heart-shaped cutter, cut biscuits. Decorate them with a lavender bud on top. Spread a little oil on the baking sheet and place it on top while making the wish you want for your loved one. Bake at 160° Celsius in the oven for about 25 minutes until golden and hard.

A bag with dried lavender, dried flowers of rosemary, and chopped German iris root can refresh the mind and body during long journeys.

Lavender is considered a masculine herb. Mercury is its ruler. It belongs to the element of air and with its mercurial action is fast and effective. It is an excellent choice for magic pillows or pouches.

In magic, it is often used in love spells. They say that paper rubbed with lavender is great for writing a love message, while clothes that have the scent of lavender or a bag of lavender on the skin, attract a lover. Rumour has it that the scent of lavender generally attracts men and prostitutes who often used its essential oil or water to attract customers but also for protection against them; since it acts as a shield against abuse. Lavender is very much associated with love, while it is believed that if you want to know how much your lover loves you, you can put lavender twigs in the pages of a book. After a while, they will reveal with their perfume how much your beloved loves you. Another "recipe" says that, for love to flourish in the room, you can sprinkle rosemary, lavender essential oil, and patchouli on a mixture of lavender flowers, rose petals, and German iris root. If you place these plants next to your bedroom door by opening and closing the door, its scent will be spread in the room and love will bloom.

It is said that the plant is so strong that if someone depressed, only by looking at it, all their sadness and sorrows will go away, and joy will return to their life. The smell of lavender gives longevity and it is said that we should smell it as often as possible! In magick, it is also used in healing mixtures as it protects against the evil eye while it is added to purifying baths.

Apart from its connection with love magic, in the Renaissance, it was believed that lavender along with rosemary could help a woman maintain her chastity. According to popular tradition, the girl who wanted to remain pure had to crush dried lavender over her head.

The gift of the flowers
Bach Flower Remedies

Dr. Edward Bach was a British Physician, who began to see disease as an end product; a final stage; a physical manifestation of unhappiness, fear, and worry. He, therefore, began to look to nature to find healing flowers. Over a period of years, Dr. Bach found 38 healing flowers and plants that with the right preparation became the 38 Bach Flower Remedies. These Remedies are enough to remove all negative emotional problems.
We will analyse the next group of flowers which concerns the:

Excessive interest in the welfare of others

Helen C. Bakopoulou
Bach remedies certified Therapist
email: bakoelen@gmail.com

Photo Canva database

GROUP 4

EXCESSIVE INTEREST IN THE WELFARE OF OTHERS

1. BEECH= Lack of Understanding, Critical Mood

Individuals criticize the mistakes of others without compassion or leniency. They are arrogant, intolerant, and very disciplined with themselves. They have sharp tongue. They only accept those who agree with their opinion. By taking the remedy, they develop understanding, leniency, tolerance, and love. They forgive.

2. CHICORY= Cautiousness, overprotectiveness

Individuals are overprotective of their loved ones and show excessive concern for their welfare. But they expect reciprocation, otherwise, they get hurt. They get involved in everything. They use secret manipulations to get control of the family. The role of the "mummy" who, if things don't go her way, falls sick. Once they get the remedy, they begin to respect others and their choices in life. They feel loved.

3. ROCK WATER = Denial, Perfectionism

Individuals are hard on themselves, self-limiting, and dogmatic. Inflexible. They live like hermits. They renounce the joys of life and sex. They seek to be a good example for others. When they take the remedy, they adapt to the present with an open mind and accept the joys of life. They evolve.

4. VINE= Authoritarian, Controlling

Such individuals are very ambitious, and confident of their abilities, with a tendency to impose themselves with authoritarianism. They strive to gain power and authority. They could become very dictatorial. Often they are strict parents at home. When they get the remedy, they become wise leaders or teachers, inspiring others rather than controlling them. They guide the weaker ones to find their own path.

5. VERVAIN=Verbal Supporter of Ideas

Individuals feel excessive enthusiasm and over-excitement in trying to convince others of their ideas and ideals. They feel like missionaries and try to save others. They are outspoken, tireless, and courageous. By taking the remedy, the anxiety subsides, and they become more diplomatic and discreet and do not interfere. They allow others to have their own opinions and their own truth.

Norse Mythology

The Apples of Idun

When the glaciers retreated at the end of the last ice age, northern Europe was a dangerous place. The gods, called Aesir, however, were the hope of the world as they were young and beautiful.

The early giants who lived in Jotunheim were envious of the gods. They were ready to attack at the slightest sign of weakness.

The gods saw the chaos around them and created Midgard, a garden in the middle of the earth. One day Odin, the father of the gods, with Hoenir, the bright sun god, and Loki, the fire god, were walking in Midgard. There they saw two trees: the ash and the elm. From each tree they carved a trunk in human form. Odin gave the logs souls. Hoenir gave them the power of movement and the gifts of the senses. Loki gave them blood and the spark of life. Thus were created the first man and the first woman; everybody else descended from them.

Then the gods decided to build a house for themselves. They crossed the wide river Ifing, whose waters never froze, to reach the wide plains of Intawold, high above Midgard. In the centre of this magnificent and sacred place they built Asgard, the palace of the gods.

Imaginarium |12

In this beautiful city there was to be neither quarrels nor bloodshed. There would be harmony as long as the gods ruled. Aesir also built the rainbow bridge, Bifrost, so that they could travel to Midgard and return.

Iduna lived in Asgard. She was the wife of Bragi, the god of poetry, and was the guardian of the golden apples of youth. The gods of Asgard did not remain young naturally: they could grow old, as mortals do. But they remained young and strong by eating apples from Iduna's magic chest.

The giants longed to eat the golden apples of youth, but Iduna never left Asgard and the apples remained safe in her magic chest. When Iduna took an apple from the chest and gave it to a god, another apple would magically appear to take its place. The gods were so sure of their eternal youth.

One day Odin, Hoenir and Loki set out on a journey to Midgard, as they often did to check what the people they had created were doing.

By evening the gods were tired and hungry, so they killed an ox and started a fire to roast it. After resting for a while, Odin reached out for some meat. To his disappointment it was still raw.

The gods stoked the fire and added more wood. They waited for a while until they were sure the meat was ready to eat. Once again Odin leaned forward over the blazing fire and tried to cut a piece. But the meat was still as raw as if it had never been near the fire.

As the ox was large, Odin, Hoenir and Loki agreed to the eagle's suggestion, thinking there was plenty of food for all of them. Then the flames of the fire leapt up and, in a few seconds, the meat was roasted. Odin cut the meat into juicy pieces and the gods were ready to eat when the eagle flew down from the tree. To their shock, it grabbed almost all of the meat, leaving them with only a few pieces.

Loki, irritated, grabbed a stick and tried to hit the eagle to get it to drop some of the food. But the eagle was actually the mountain giant, Thiashi, in disguise and possessed great magical powers. The wand stuck firmly in the eagle's back and in Loki's hands.

The eagle soared into the air and the helpless god flew into the sky with his feet tapping on the treetops.

'Let me go!' cried Loki.

'Not until you promise to do something for me,' cried Thiassi. He flew up and down and through the trees, so that Loki's pain increased. 'When I free you,' Thiassi continued, 'don't say anything about this to the other gods. When you return to Asgard, I want you to lure Iduna to walk to Midgard, so that I can take her and the chest with the golden apples of youth'. Loki was horrified, but his pain was such that he vowed to do as Thiashi demanded. Then Thiassi released him and walked back into the forest to rejoin Odin and Hoenir. He told them nothing of his promise and they were surprised that he had escaped the eagle so easily. After a few days the three gods completed their journey and returned to Asgard.

Imaginarium |13

It so happened that Iduna's husband, Bragi, was away from Asgard and she was left alone. He travelled playing the lute and singing his poetry.

Loki went to see Iduna and asked her if she would give him one of her golden apples. As always, Iduna opened the magic chest and, pulling out an apple, gave it to Loki. Immediately another apple appeared in the chest.

Instead of eating the apple, Loki looked at it, turned it over and held it up to the light. Iduna was confused. 'Is something wrong?' she asked.

'No,' replied Loki, 'but I wonder. I thought there were no more apples like these, but only this morning I saw some like them down in the people's country.'

At first Iduna laughed and would not believe him, but Loki seemed so sure that the apples he had seen were exactly the same as Iduna's and he agreed to take her to show her. Iduna followed Loki out of the walls of Asgard with her apple chest so they can compare the apples.

Loki drove her farther and farther away from the safety of Asgard, and suddenly he hid, and Iiduna was left alone. Now she realized that she had been deceived and turned to run back to Asgard, but it was too late. The giant Thiashi, still disguised as an eagle, grabbed her with his claws and carried Iduna and the chest of apples to his place in the mountains.

Loki secretly returned to Asgard and told no one what had happened. At first, Iduna was not missing. Everyone thought she had gone off with her husband Bragi. Then gradually the effect of the golden apples began to fade. Lines appeared on the beautiful young faces and their hair began to turn grey. Aesir became ill and ached with the pains of age. They searched for Iduna throughout Asgard, but could not find her. They asked each other and found that Iduna was last seen with Loki. Odin sent for Loki, who was so frightened that he confessed how he had betrayed Iduna to Thiashi. All the gods were enraged and threatened Loki with immediate death if he did not save Iduna and take back the golden apples of youth. Loki was getting older himself, so he knew he would have to get over his fear of Thiashi. He begged Freya, the goddess of love, to lend him her disguise as a hawk as that way Thiashi would not suspect him.

Freya gave Loki her hawk wings and he flew to the mountain house of the giants. Luckily, Thiassi was away fishing in the north and Iduna was sitting alone with her apple chest at her side.

Loki circled around the sad and lonely goddess sitting in the castle and transformed her and the chest into a small nut. He grabbed it with his claws, flapped his wings and flew as fast as he could towards the safety of Asgard's walls. But he did not escape unnoticed. Thiashi returned from fishing in time to see the hawk fly off towards the horizon. Recognizing the hawk's wings as a disguise for the gods, he quickly pulled on his eagle wings and flew off in pursuit of the hawk.

The huge eagle easily beat the smaller hawk. Loki, weakened by old age, had to muster all his strength to keep ahead. Finally he flew exhausted over the walls of Asgard and fell to the ground.

Meanwhile, the gods had lined up along the walls of their magnificent city, watching the sky intently for Loki's return. Seeing the eagle in pursuit, they piled wood on the battlements. As soon as Loki crossed the walls, the gods lit the wood and Thiashi was caught in the flames and smoke. Choking and blinded, he fell to the ground inside Asgard and was quickly killed by the angry gods.

Loki and Iduna returned to their true form and the gods were able to eat the golden apples of youth once again. How happy the gods were to see their wrinkles and grey hair disappear and their youth and beauty return.

Odin ordered that Thiassi's eyes be taken to the heavens and turned into twinkling stars to remember him. The respect they showed the dead giant tempered the anger of his brothers and caused no further trouble.

Hypotheticals

By Japneet Chandoak

In between feeling everything and nothing,
I find myself standing in front of the traffic lights,
Waiting to 'accidentally' run into you and call it fate,
As if my whole life I didn't plan for you.
The lights go green but I don't move,
I can see figures approaching but none of them is you,
But when we finally meet and I look into your eyes,
Can we call it love at first sight?
I'll get you flowers and everything more,
Hold your hand when we walk down the streets,
Make you happy till sadness is unknown,
Tell me, am I not the dream?
And if I could stop with hypotheticals
Then this wouldn't be a hypothetical.
The traffic lights are red again,
And I finally catch your face at the opposing end,
The stillness stings,
Notice me, let me breathe you back to life.
What if,
What if,
What if we finally meet?
The lights are green again, come near me,
This moment is my fever dream.
Watch your silhouette pass by,
Call your name like I haven't every night,
But you're lost in the crowd like every version of me.
On the other road now,
You're as fleeting as this moment,
I look at the traffic lights, red yellow green,
None in the shades of you,
Love is a little lonely.

You
By Japneet Chandoak

Say you want this,
To be loved.
Say you need him, to feel alive.
But when you stop talking, his silence echoes in your mind.
You miss him in November,
In the midst of cold mornings, you yearn for his sweater.
The one which kept you warm during those freezing nights,
The one lying torn to shreds by your bedside.
I asked you, when you felt most full of life,
'Drenching my pillows, rain pouring from my eyes," you replied.
Addicted to this pain, the one you keep running away from,
When in truth, it's all you're running to.
You can't feel empty,
Nothingness could never save you.
So you cry alone, trying to feel alive.
When July comes, the sun blinds you,
You never look at it, for you may become see-through.
You wish to be this mystery,
When in reality you're on the poster of lucidity.
Say you're everything you want to be,
But it's never enough.
You hear screaming but it's not your own,
Worried, you answer the door,
Only to find it's a 17-year-old girl in tears,
You look at her face,
You're looking at you.

Find out more on Instagram at @whatif_xx and on linktr.ee/japneetchandoak

Wheel of the Year

CELEBRATING Ostara

On March 20 the Sun passes into Aries, marking the vernal equinox and the beginning of the festival of Ostara. In this article, you will find different ways to celebrate the Sabbath depending on your tradition.

Decorate Your Altar

The festival of Ostara marks the beginning of spring and the warmest part of the year and is a time when we celebrate New Life and by extension every new beginning. A few days before the festival you can prepare your altar to welcome spring.

One idea is to use spring colours, such as shades of yellow and other pastel colours found in your garden flowers. Don't forget green, of course. You can put coloured tablecloths or candles in the above colours. Natural objects such as eggs, rabbits, and also flowers that symbolize the fertility of spring are very good to have on your altar. You can also put some small statues of gods in black and white or symbols of the Sun and Moon which during the vernal equinox symbolize the balance of light and darkness. You can also put symbols of Aries or even symbols of the heart chakra.

It is very important in your altar to have lots of spring flowers such as dandelion, echinacea and daffodils, hyacinths, narcissi, tulips, and lilies or violets are some of the magical spring flowers that symbolize growth, abundance, transformation, and fertility.

Another idea is to put a basket of eggs which are also symbols of fertility, and you can also add a cup of milk or honey. Milk represents baby animals that have just been born and honey is known as a symbol of abundance.

Decorate your altar with crystals such as rose quartz, moonstone, and aquamarine, and don't forget to include the element of fire by either adding candles as mentioned above, or burning incense in a cauldron.

As you decorate and get ready for spring reflect on what you would like to create for yourself in the year ahead. What seeds would you like to plant and what are your intentions? What part of your life would you like to rejuvenate? What parts of your life would you like to balance on the day when light and darkness are in perfect balance?

Connect to the Source

After you have prepared your altar a walk in nature where you will observe the new life. This is the best way to connect with the energy of the sabbath and by extension spring. Dare to take off your shoes and step on the ground as this technique connects and grounds you. You can also do earth meditation where you can sit or lie down on the ground and try to connect all your senses to the earth while breathing lightly through your nose, and exhaling through your mouth. Smell the earth and feel its moisture and all the power of the flowers and plants in bloom. Feel the cool breeze and allow yourself to connect with the rhythms of nature. Once you come into total relaxation visualize a golden light passing through your body from the third eye warming your head and descending throughout your body. As the light passes through your body, visualize the return of the warm, spiritual Sun into your life.

Welcome the Deities

There are many deities that have been associated with spring and depending on your cultural background you can celebrate the Ostara with cultural variations.

For example, in parts of Africa, they honour the Asase Yaa, an earth goddess who brings new life in the spring. The Ashanti people of Ghana honour her at the festival of Durbar alongside her husband Nyame, the sky god who brings rain to the fields. The deity has no official temple but is honoured in the fields where the crops grow and in homes where she is honoured as the goddess of fertility and the womb.

Another deity is Cybele who is considered the mother goddess of Rome. Her rituals included priestesses leading devotees in rituals that included ecstatic music, drumming, and dancing. There is also evidence of mystical rites that were more orgiastic in nature. Today many people still honour Cybele not in the same way as in antiquity however there are groups such as Maetrum of Cybele who honour her as the Mother Goddess and patroness of women.

James Doyle Penrose - Freya and the Necklace, circa 1890

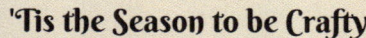

A popular fertility goddess is Freya who returns to earth in the spring to bring back the beauty of nature. She wears an astonishing necklace, the Brisingamen which symbolizes the fire of the sun. Freya as Odin's wife was often called upon to assist in births or marriages as well as being the guardian of women who want to have a child. If you are one of them, ask her for help on this day.

A strong and masculine deity of fertility is Osiris of Egypt, the king of all the gods of Egypt. According to legend, he was a lover (and brother!) of Isis, who died and was reborn. According to legend, he became the first Pharaoh of Egypt and taught mankind the secrets of agriculture and farming, and is also believed, based on the legend, to have brought civilization to the world. His death by his brother Set is a very big event in Egyptian magic and worship.

Another goddess associated with the arts, teaching, wisdom, and spring is the Indian goddess Saraswati, who is honoured with prayers and music every spring and is usually represented holding a lotus in bloom and the sacred Vedas.

Finally, it is worth mentioning Eostre, a goddess whose roots are mysteriously lost in Germanic mythology, yet her stories are passed down from generation to generation. No one knows if this deity actually existed in any religion or mythology, while many believe that she is simply the etymological proof for Easter.

'Tis the Season to be Crafty

If you have children at home you can celebrate spring with various craft projects such as dying eggs naturally (you'll find several ideas on YouTube), a tradition that is quite common in Orthodox Christianity, and you can also make crafts such as making a flower wreath, seed bags or seed greeting cards to give to your loved ones or even start a mini greenhouse. Another fun project for the sabbath is to make a decorative tree with twigs that you have decorated with foam eggs, after previously colouring them and decorating them with various ribbons.

Cast this Circle

If you are alone and just want to feel the spiritual essence of the holiday you can do a ritual to connect with the forces of the universe on this powerful and energetic day.

You will need three candles, one green, one yellow and one purple. A bowl of sugar or honey and a bowl of milk.

Preferably go out into nature. Cast a circle and light the green candle that symbolizes the earth blossoming. Say the following words:

The wheel of the year turns once again,
and the spring equinox arrives.
Light and darkness are equal,
and the ground begins to change.
The earth awakens from its slumber,
and new life sparks forth once more.

Then light the yellow candle representing the sun and say:

The sun is getting closer and closer to us,
welcoming the earth with its welcoming rays.
Light and darkness are equal,
and the sky is filled with light and warmth.
The sun warms the earth beneath our feet,
and gives life to all in its wake.

Finally, light the purple candle which represents the sacred forces of life. Focus on the invisible forces of the universe around you and within you and say:

Spring is here! We are grateful for it!
The Divine is present everywhere,
in the cool fall of a rainstorm,
in the tiny buds of a flower,

Imaginarium |21

*in the feather of a newborn chick,
in the fertile fields waiting to be planted,
in the sky above us,
and the earth beneath us.
We thank the universe for all it has to offer us,
and we are blessed to live this day.
Welcome, life! Welcome, light! Welcome, spring!*

Visualize and meditate on the three flames and what they symbolize. Mix honey with milk and pour it on the earth as an offering saying:

*I make this offering to the earth,
As thanks for the many blessings I have received,
And those I shall some day receive.*

Stay for a few minutes afterwards and feel the earth at your feet and the sun on your face. Feel in total balance with the darkness and light within you and seek harmony in every step you take.

*(This ritual is by By Patti Wigington. Check more great rituals and articles on www.learnreligions.com)

Make it a Feast!

So whatever your cultural or spiritual background, the festival of the vernal equinox offers so many alternatives to celebrate it. Don't forget, of course, to combine all the above with delicious treats like hot cross buns and of course, colourful salads, eggs, and flower cakes!

Blessed Ostara!

Wellbeing

FLOWER POWER
in your May Day Bouquet

May Day is a European festival of ancient origins (Roman festival: Floralia, and Greek festival: Anthesteria) marking the beginning of summer, usually celebrated on 1 May. Festivities may also be held the night before, known as May Eve. Traditions often include gathering wildflowers and green branches, weaving floral garlands, crowning a May Queen, and setting up a Maypole, May Tree or May Bush, around which people dance. Make a May Day garland, bouquet, or wreath using the Flower Power to bring magic into your life this Spring!

Purple Lily
Spontaneity
If you carry guilt about falling into a routine of no return, you need to shake up your life a bit. The purple lily will give you the motivation to live spontaneously and joyfully and feel as calm as ever. Begin to step out of the protective zone you have created!

Tulip
Grace
Happy thoughts will lead you to have the right attitude. You will inspire admiration for the graciousness with which you deal with everything, even the most difficult situations. A sweet charm will make your face shine like a bouquet of beautiful tulips.

Pansies
Opportunities without limits
Brings out your innate talent to achieve your best. You will be encouraged to put aside any false impressions you have of yourself and your true desires will be unleashed. Your dreams will begin to take shape.

Primula veris (cowslip)
Self-esteem
Do you feel unloved? Accept yourself as it is, showing leniency to the parts of your character that you usually criticize strongly. If you can manage to love yourself even a little more, others will love you more too. So what are you waiting for? Start right away!

Bell Flower
Natural Energy
Brings more natural energy into your daily life. Maybe take up a sport? Start gently, with walking or swimming, 2-3 times a week and gradually increase. As your body exercises, your mood will improve and you will find your balance.

Violet
Friendship
A new era of togetherness begins. Find the time and dedicate it to friends, relatives, or neighbours. Offer help, show your sympathy to those close to you, and accept theirs. You will immediately feel good and expand your social circle.

Lilium
Peace
It's natural to feel powerless in the face of all the bad things happening around you. Lily will help you to start making changes. Start with yourself first. Find your inner peace and make peace with yourself so you can help others.

Iris
Acceptance
Feeling different from others or that you don't belong anywhere? The iris encourages you to appreciate your diversity. Use your intuition and change your life to find the most suitable job, people, and places that will inspire you to a better future.

Amaryllis
Sexuality
If you have had unpleasant experiences try to shake them off and find deep down inside what truly pleases you. If you have been trapping your sexual energy, you will slowly release it and you will definitely feel more creative.

Echinacea
Empowerment
Find the power that lies within you and step forward powerfully. Only you can help yourself. So take life into your own hands and don't forget that every difficulty makes you more mature. This way, you will face problems more easily and enjoy your life.

Daisy
Bliss
To achieve bliss, you must learn to safeguard your environment. Calm down and examine how you really feel inside and where there may be tension or pain. Pay no attention and mentally drift off to a calmer place. You will feel wonderful.

Poppy
Positive Disposition
It will help you to embrace the positive aspects of your character and minimize the negative ones. You will learn to discern the good more easily even in the most difficult situations. If you truly love what you do, poppy will lead you to ultimate happiness.

Carnation
Deep Love
Express your love with white carnations. If you admire someone, don't hesitate to tell them, and treat people you care about affectionately without hesitation. If you prefer some other colour, it's no different. It's just that white also brings good luck.

Chrysanthemum
Optimism
The golden flower can only bring joy; facing everything with optimism, you will surely enjoy not only happy days but also success. In Japan, there is even a "Happiness Festival" every year which is celebrated with chrysanthemums.

Our Friends... The Trees

According to ancient traditions and beliefs, trees have impressive metaphysical properties, as well as healing energy, and through specific methods, we can "communicate" with them. All around us, we have a plethora of such silent "friends" that accompany us in our evolution.

Researchers claim that trees, through the exchange of energy, are so emotionally connected to humans that their friendship knows no boundaries. This was proven by the oscilloscopes, which recorded the trees' distress when their 'protégé' was harmed, even though they were miles apart. They also claim that as "ethereal" entities they can give their irrefutable testimony to an event they "saw" or experienced, that they can read our thoughts and intentions beforehand, and even have musical preferences! In folk tradition, trees protect us from evil eye and bad luck. We can all, therefore, have such a precious "friend", provided only that our relationship is characterized by mutual love and care. Thus, we ought to heal our tree friend, if necessary, or thoughtfully, hang an amulet on it, so that it may be protected.

Instructions for "contact"
Nature feels us

The Tibetan Lamas revealed that even a small tree in our backyard is inextricably linked to the fate of our family. In Finland and Lithuania, even today, every child who comes into the world gets his or her own tree and grows up with it. It is not uncommon to see pictures in those places where a child, on the way to school, hugs the tree and spends a few minutes with it. The same is repeated when they are back home. Taoism and all the shamanistic traditions - but also many philosophers such as Goethe and Steiner, and even naturalists - insist that trees have extraordinary properties and that the exchange of energy between two beings in the universe is the reason why all the miraculous things happen. In their deeply held belief, this proves the unity of everything.

Moreover, the scientific world was shocked by the revelation made by two scientific researchers and authors of the book 'The secret life of plants', Peter Tompkins and Christopher Bird, who through experiments and aided by advances in technology discovered that trees have sensitive nervous systems! They feel love, hate, joy, fear, pain, agitation and have a multitude of other reactions due to corresponding stimuli.

There are many methods to develop friendship between a human and a tree, but here we will rely mainly on the Taoist tradition. All, however, are based on the natural attraction of communication that will precede any process. So let your instincts guide you in choosing your own friend.

If no particular tree comes to mind, start with the one in your home or neighbourhood and, if there is none or none that actually inspires you, head for the park.

It is very important to remember that "choose" here has a two-way meaning. The basic premise is mutual liking so you have to be open to the tree to choose you as well. We need to understand, almost feel the plant "telling" us that we have become friends of this level.

Later we can ask it very specific questions about matters of concern, and get answers.

Of course, you can't get anything if you don't give, so a low-key "talk" with our new companion, a gentle touch with our hand, or even sitting with our backs resting on its trunk, and a little water on its roots as a sign of offering, should precede our request.

The well-known Taoist Mantak Chia suggests the following method for developing communication with a tree and exchanging our energy with its energy.

Imaginarium |28

1 Stand in front of it with a straight spine and a calm spirit, without any grasping tendencies or demanding expectations, so as not to block the plant's nervous system in its attempt to defend itself. With respect and a willingness to exchange, embrace the trunk without touching it and remain in a waiting posture for a while until the tree itself "talks" to you. A variation of this method is touching the trunk with the palms of your hands or placing them a few centimetres away from it (yang energy of the sky).

2 Soon you will feel the energy of the plant in your hands and from there throughout your body.

3 Then visualize the negative energy coming out of your hands and your whole body and going towards your new friend and from there, through its roots (yin energy), towards the earth, which is an "empty container", and disappearing. The process also can be done by coordinating the breath. From this point on, the tree will know almost everything about you. Repeat the process, if possible, at regular intervals.

12 Helpers

... for love

Apple tree: "Opening" of the love life promises the apple tree, with its juicy fruits, which signal the awakening of passion. It communicates with the heart chakra and is best placed on the southwest side of the house.

Chestnut tree: Works in favour of increasing the sex drive and fertility. According to folk belief, if one kisses a woman under a chestnut tree, she has a good chance of getting pregnant soon. It still gives joy and encouragement in all areas of life.

Magnolia: If, again, you want to "welcome" a new love in your life, get a magnolia and say goodbye to loneliness for good.

Birch: It symbolizes the power of love and guarantees the return of happiness and reconciliation. It gives strength, health, and longevity.

Acacia: Symbolizes pure love and will not let you fall into the hands of someone not good for you.

Fir: Ideal for all those who are in relationship with younger romantic partners or are married to much younger spouses. Promotes faithfulness and loyalty.

... for the "evil eye"

Linden: To remove the "evil eye" is a miraculous solution. Linden (or a small bundle of leaves) banishes all the negative energy coming from the evil eye.

Elm: It protects against gossip and jinx.

... for money and luck

Almond tree: For money, loans, and handling. If you bury a little money in its roots, it brings prosperity. It can also help you develop your divination skills.

Juniper: It brings health, attracts money, and in "partnership" with a pine tree next to it, it renews energy.

Oak: Suitable for all those who want to gain power.

Fern: Brings, in general, good luck.

Kitchen Witchery

Meeting Andreea Gagiu
Thyme to Slice and Dice

Photo by Andreea Gagiu, all rights reserved

Ireland-based food photographer and recipe developer, Andreea Gagiu talks to us about her love of food and the art of creating a visual story with it.

Interview to Anastasia Diakidi

A.D. Andreea, thank you for being here. You live in Ireland, a beautiful country and you are from Romania, is that correct? I would like you to tell us a few words about yourself and your photographic journey and how your culture has played a role – maybe- in your artistic expression.

A.G. Hello everyone. Thank you so much for having me here.

Yes, I was born and raised in Romania and moved to beautiful Ireland nearly 8 years ago. I am the face behind @thymetosliceanddice which started 3 years ago. It's been quite a journey and I loved every minute of it.

My first photo was posted during the first pandemic lockdown. Looking back now it was not my best work but it made me ambitious to study and get good at it. I spend a lot of time learning camera settings, light, food styling, and how to create powerful visual storytelling.
I want my food to take people on a journey of memory, emotion, and taste.

A.D. What made you choose this field of photography?

A.G. Food always played a very important part in my life. When I think of memories throughout my life a lot of them include food in some way: my mom in the kitchen baking a dessert on Sundays, my grandmothers making doughnuts, and birthday cakes, and sharing meals with family and friends. My love for cooking and baking made me choose this type of photography.

A.D. Do you mix elements and influences from both countries?

A.G. Yes, I like to mix elements from both countries and their cultures. It makes my photography stand out from the crowd.

A.D. What are the elements of a successful food photo?

A.G. There are so many elements to consider.
In my opinion the most important are:
  -the subject
  -lighting: soft diffused natural light is the best
  -composition: how the elements are arranged, use different textures and colours
  -tell a story: where the dish came from, how it was made, who made it.

A.D. In the last few years, more and more people turn to food photography, why do you think this is happening?

Photo by Andreea Gagiu, all rights reserved

Imaginarium |31

I think it s because social media plays a very important part in our lives nowadays.
We all want to share things we saw, places we went, and our experiences with friends and followers. Food photography is a way for people to express and share their cooking experiences and passion with others.

A.D. Any tips for someone who would like to start with food photography? Or simply anyone who would like to take nice food photos?

A.G. The best tip that I can give and it worked for me is to study the work of professional photographers. Take the time and study their photos and the details that you like about them and incorporate them into your work.
There are so many free resources online shared by some amazing photographers that can help with the learning process.
You don't need to invest in the most expensive equipment to start; just take your camera and start practicing. Be creative and unique.

A.D What story do you want to tell with your pictures? What "message" do you want to convey?

A.G. My message is that anyone can bake beautiful and delicious cakes from the comfort of their kitchen.

By sharing my food photography and recipes I hope to give others the same joy and happiness I feel and I am hopeful people will try and make them. There is nothing better than a home-baked dessert.

A.D. Do you do collaborations? Where could people find you?

A.G. That is definitely something I am looking forward to. People can find me on my Instagram page: @thymetosliceanddice for collaborations, questions or just to say hi.

A.D. Nowadays, everyone is in a hurry and people do not enjoy food preparation or they don't even cook at all. I believe that this for you is different. What food means to you? What would you advise people to do to find a lost connection to food?

A.G. The time I spend in the kitchen is fun and relaxing. I have a chance to be creative and express myself differently with every recipe I try. It's so much more than just food on a plate: it's passion. Put your apron on, grab a rolling pin, and bake! It will make you happy.

A.D Thank you so much for sharing space with us. I wish you all the best with all your future endeavours.

Photos by Andreea Gagiu, all rights reserved

Recipes by Andreea Gagiu

Lemon and poppyseed muffin

These lemon and poppyseed muffins are moist, soft, fluffy, and topped with a delicious raspberry buttercream. A very easy recipe that can be made by anyone.

Raspberry buttercream:
75 g frozen raspberry
150 g icing sugar
75 g soft butter
pinch of salt

Blend the defrosted raspberries into a puree and strain out any pulp and seeds through a fine strainer.
In a bowl mix the soft butter with a pinch of salt until it s soft and creamy.
Add half of the sugar and fruit puree and mix just a little bit to combine. Continue adding the rest of the sugar and fruit puree and mix on low speed just until the buttercream is light and fluffy. Keep in the fridge until ready to use.

Muffins:
200 g soft butter   *1 teaspoon baking powder*
200 g flour   *3 tablespoons of lemon juice*
200 g sugar   *3 tablespoons of poppy seed*
4 eggs   *Zest from one lemon*

In a bowl, mix the soft sugar with the butter for 4-5 minutes until it s light and fluffy.

Add the eggs one by one, making sure you mix well each and every one.

In a different bowl, combine all the dry ingredients: flour, baking powder, poppy seeds, and lemon zest.

Put the wet ingredients over, add the lemon juice, and mix well.

Bake the muffins in the preheated oven at 170° or until golden- the time varies on each oven. Keep an eye on them.

Decorate them when they are cooled down or serve them simply. Enjoy!

Raspberry Panna Cotta

Panna cotta is one of those simple but sophisticated desserts that everyone should try. Infused with elderflower syrup and topped with raspberry coulis it makes a stunning dessert perfect for any occasion.

400ml double cream
250 ml milk
3-4 tablespoons of elderflower syrup
50 g sugar
5 gelatine leaves
Raspberry coulis

Soak the gelatine leaves in very cold water for about 5 minutes.

In a small saucepan add the cream, milk, and sugar.

Gently heat stirring until it's just about to boil. Remove from the heat, let it cool down for a few minutes, and add the gelatine leaves removing the excess water from them.

Stir until it has completely dissolved and add the elderflower syrup. If you like the taste you can definitely add more.

Pour the panna cotta into the glasses. Leave in the fridge to firm. After one hour you can add the raspberry coulis and leave it again in the fridge for a few hours.

Raspberry coulis:
300 g frozen raspberries
3 tablespoons of sugar
lemon zest

Put the frozen raspberries, sugar, and lemon zest in a small pan over medium heat. Let it boil for a few minutes.

Once it cools down blend it into a puree. If you don't like the seeds you can press them through a sieve and remove them. You will have smooth and silky coulis. Pour it over the panna cotta and let it set in the fridge. Enjoy!

Lemon, basil, and redcurrant bundt cake

This lemon and basil bundt cake it's a unique dessert that will definitely impress.
If you never tried using fresh basil in a cake you will be surprised.

250 g soft butter
250 g flour
225 g caster sugar
4 large eggs
1 and 1/2 teaspoons of baking powder
pinch of salt
Zest from two lemons
4 tablespoons of frozen red currant
2-3 tablespoons of chopped fresh basil

Preheat oven to 170 degrees.

Generously butter your bundt pan with melted butter making sure you get into all the corners.

In a bowl mix the butter, sugar, lemon zest, and fresh basil for a few minutes until light and fluffy. Add the eggs one by one mixing well after each one.

Imaginarium |34

Sift the flour with salt and baking powder into the bowl and mix to combine everything.
Pour the cake batter into the bunt pan and sprinkle the red currants all over.
Bake for 40 min but it might need longer.

When you think it s done try it by sticking a toothpick in the middle. If it comes out dry it's done.
Let it cool down for 5 minutes and remove it from the pan. Enjoy!

Photos by Andreea Gagiu, all rights reserved

Imaginarium |35

Sabbath

BELTANE & WALPURGIS NIGHT

The festival of fire and magic

Beltane is the seasonal festival that marks the transition to the warmer months of the year and is one of the most important and widespread holidays according to the pagan Wheel of the Year.

Beltane celebrates the beginning of summer and is often called Mayday since it is celebrated on May 1. The celebration historically and in today's pagan tradition, is associated with the element of fire. Big bonfires are lit at the big Beltane festivals, both for the celebration itself as well as the ritual required.

One such ritual is found in 10th-century Irish sources which mentions cattle around fires where people chant in order to bring protection to their animal in the coming months. Fire is generally considered lucky and protective, which is why many people walk around it or jump over it, a tradition that is still held today during the celebrations of Beltane and May Day in many parts of Europe.

Another important feature is the feast with offerings to the gods and the spirits for a fruitful summer. Regarding the origin of the festival there is a theory that it is connected with the Sun-God called Belanus, god of Celtic mythology. However, there are few sources and historical references about this deity and its association with the early festivals. "Bel" basically means passage, a small gap, while "taine" is the old Irish word for fire.

Another coincidence or connection is the ancient Greek Anthestiria which was celebrated at the beginning of May and was dedicated to the goddess Demeter and her daughter Persephone who that month was coming back from the Underworld and ascending to Earth. Similarly, in ancient Rome, there were festivals called "rosyllia" which were maintained by the Byzantine Emperors later.

According to tradition, the windows and doors are decorated with magic wreaths for the festival. These are not just for decorative reasons but they were believed to offer protection to the home, and in this way the fairies were appeased. In addition to flowers, they also decorated twigs on the doors because they believed that their cows would have good milk production. Even today in Beltane we see similar traditions such as the crowning of May Queen, the dance around the maypole as well as the decoration of bushes and wreaths.

Same as on Halloween, the feast of All Saints, on Beltane it is believed that the veil between the two worlds becomes very thin. Traditions, beliefs and prejudices have been associated with May Day since ancient times.

The eve of May Day is also called Walpurgis night, a night that is inextricably linked to the magical tradition and the sabbaths of witches. The name of the festival comes from St. Valpurga, an English nun and missionary who was sent to Germany and founded a monastery for monks and nuns. Gradually, she spread the Christian faith in pagan Germany, and also became known for her healing abilities as well as her mission against witchcraft. But how is a feast associated with the gatherings of witches connected with the Saint who prosecuted them? It is not known how the identification took place, but in all likelihood the pagan festivals became entangled with the Christian ones and then were identified.

St. Valpurga was associated with the feast when her relics were transferred to her monastery in German Eichstätt on May 1 and her canonization occurred.

The Sabbath of the witches, on the other hand, that takes place

Imaginarium |37

Another German tradition, the ankenschnitt, wants people to burn last year's beddings and leave offerings to spirits such as honey, butter, and bread. Also, the dew is considered to have magical properties and whoever bathes with it or washes their face will have fresh and clean skin.

Although Beltane and its popularity is gradually declining with the new era, neo-pagans still follow the tradition and celebrate it widely. In the context of cultural revival, pagans revive old customs but also add new ones to the modern festival.

every Beltane Eve started from the German tradition. It was believed that witches from all over the world gathered every year at the top of Mount Brocken, where they performed the magical rituals of spring under the moonlight. The first written reference to this belief comes in the 17th century from Johannes Praetorious's The Blocksberg Performance. But the wide spread of myths about witches and their rituals came in the 19th-20th century, probably from the influence of Goethe's Faust. The colonization of paganism gave Walpurgis Night an orgiastic tone as it was believed that witches had orgies with the devil.

The coincidence of the feast of the Saint with the feast of May Day, led to the celebrations taking place on the first day of May in most of northern Europe. In various places, people went a step further, and so for their protection against witches and evil that were walking free that night -as it is happening on All Hallows Eve-, they lit large fires and made noise or disguised themselves to cast out evil spirits.

Imaginarium |38

BASIC ASTROLOGY COURSE
by VASILIOS TAKOS

Study the *Principles of Basic astrology* and reach for the stars!

- ★ for beginners, but also for experienced astrologers
- ★ for personal or professional use
- ★ easy registration and accessibility
- ★ well structured with rich material and diagrams
- ★ pre-recorded online lessons, adaptable to each student's schedule
- ★ support to every student
- ★ graduate certification
- ★ you can start the course immediately after purchase

Why waste time? Register now!
vasiliostakos.com

You are not required to own or purchase any professional astrology software or to buy any accompanying book, as everything you need is provided within the lessons.

Elemental Magic

FIRE
The Element of Life

The four elements of fire, earth, air, and water are present all around us. The ancient Greeks believed that every living organism is made of a combination of these elements. It is no coincidence that the four elements have a place not only in the physical world but also in many religious concepts as well as in the metaphysical world. In this issue, we will explore the element of fire.

Although fire is a natural element, it has contributed to the creation of civilization, and its history is intertwined in time with the history and evolution of man.

As an element in metaphysics, it is considered dynamic as fire symbolizes masculine qualities. In astrology, fire is associated with the planets that have a hot nature, namely those of the Sun and Mars (and Jupiter in its mild and more balanced form), while the signs that correspond to it are Aries, Leo, and Sagittarius.

In Aries, we see the first spark, the one that the caveman lit and essentially started civilization. Through the sign of Leo, fire has now become constant and is used not only to help man in his basic survival but through it, man now begins to create jewellery and other objects for his personal appearance and self-expression. In Sagittarius fire is now a means for man to expand, travel and exchange knowledge with others as it is used in technology and science.

In astrology also the element of fire is associated with characteristics such as confidence, initiative, courage, boldness, strength, honesty, freedom of expression, leadership, and fearlessness. The negative characteristics of fire include arrogance, impulsiveness, impatience, selfishness, and despotism.

Imaginarium |40

As with any element, balance is everything. Fire is a powerful element that in nature we know all too well its negative effects and how destructive it can be. The same is true in human temperaments, where the element of fire also needs balance, or else the negative characteristics of the element can damage the personality and those around us.

In traditional astrology, for example, Mars, ruler of Aries, was considered to be malefic and was attributed with many evils, such as violence and destructive behaviours (when not well rated, as it is said).

In modern astrology where things are no longer black and white, we know that the martian qualities are exceptionally positive if they are balanced, and without them, a person has no self-confidence, zest for life, vitality, determination, and courage.

In tarot, the element of fire is associated with the Wands of the Minor Arcana. As in astrology, the wands are associated with the passion, enthusiasm, action, and energy of the Yang. Clearly, we see the power of willpower, justice, strength, and the virtue of truth in this suit. In Major Arcana, the element of Fire can be connected to the cards of the Emperor, the Sun, the Strength, and Temperance.

In herbalism and folk medicine, the element of fire has been associated with herbs and plants ruled by Sun and Mars. These herbs usually have thorns, such as nettles, for example, and some of them may have a very spicy taste, such as chilli peppers. In ancient medicine, those herbs were recommended when it was thought that the fire element was lacking in humans. For example, in ailments where the moist and cold element prevailed, they recommended herbs associated with the Sun or Mars to raise the heat and dryness of the body.

In crystal healing, fire-related crystals are usually orange or yellow in colour such as, for example, gold amber, fire opal, yellow, tiger's eye, and cornelian. Fire element crystals are known for their ability to stimulate psychic powers. However, these stones have as their main property to warm the spirit, energize it, increase confidence, and create comforting and uplifting feelings. They provide sunny energy to stimulate the mind, especially during winter months. In cases where the body needs strengthening and the spirit needs to find its enthusiasm, fire crystals are recommended by healers.

We see the same in homeopathy where remedies related to the element of fire such as Britannicus sol or Aurum promote the feeling of happiness and help people to feel more joyful in their daily life.

The fire element corresponds to the heart chakra. This chakra is located in the centre of your chest, between your collarbones. It's associated with love, passion, creativity, ambition, self-expression, and communication.

On the Wheel of the Year, the festival most associated with fire is Beltane. On this sabbath pagans light large bonfires where they jump over it and follow rituals associated with the return of the sun to the earth, marking the beginning of the warmest period of the year.

The fire element in witchcraft is the use of fire for magical purposes. This includes the use of candles, incense, fireplaces, torches, fire pits, bonfires, campfires, and any other form of fire used for magical purposes.

Spells and rituals associated with fire have to do with the creation of new life, the beginning of a new venture, love, and especially its sexual side, and the strengthening of health and the spirit. Also spells of weakening enemies and banishing evil beings or spirits.

Wiccans use the elements to symbolize the four directions. The four directions correspond to the four classical elements. Fire is the element that represents passion, sexuality, creativity, and power. It can be used for good or evil depending on how you use it.

Fire is the element of the north. This element is most powerful at noon when the sun is hot. For example, when casting a love spell, this will be strongest at noontime.
Noon is also a liminal hour, so magick meant to balance things is powerful at that time.
Other types of magick to use the fire element at noontime include success and money spells.

The fire element has been associated since ancient times -and by witches!- with the hearth. There is a close connection between the hearth of the home and the fire element as this is where we humans cook but we also have a more active role in this area of our home.

The most famous of the deities of the house and the hearth is of course Hestia, the Greek Goddess of Olympus. It is said that to her the humans gave the first offerings before any other God. However, she is not mentioned in many myths and there are not many stories about her. She was generally a passive deity and did not play a significant role in the lives of the Greeks, however, Hestia was always present in the home and in the public hearth. She was considered a virgin goddess and was associated with the preparation of meals and the baking of bread. She was identified with the eternal flame and in the town hall, the prytaneum, of the city there was a public temple where the eternal flame burned in her honour. The hearth was the heart of the home so the public hearth was dedicated to the goddess too and was considered to be the heart of the city. With the founding of each new city, embers from the public hearth had to be transferred to light the public hearth of the new city. The same was done when one built a new house. The fire in general, in the city or in the house, had a spiritual substance and was not supposed to be put out. It is said that if the fire in a house was extinguished, rituals of purification and renewal were followed in order to relight it. Although there was no formal worship of the goddess, she was worshipped in all homes on a daily basis and was considered sacred to every family.

A similar deity was the Roman Vesta which had a similar function and position as Hestia of the Greek Pantheon. However, the worship of Vesta was formalised and there was an order of priestesses who worshipped her in temples. The Sacred Flame symbolized the life and safety of Rome so it was always to be looked after by the so-called Vestal Virgins, the priestesses of the Vesta. Those priestesses had an oath of chastity and dedicated their lives and energy to serve the goddess for 30 years. The Sacred Fire of Vesta was rekindled every first of March after the hearth had been purged. However, a part of the flame always stayed lit - carried to safety until the hearth was cleaned, so the eternal flame never really went out. Even the ashes were considered sacred and were stored at the base of the temple and thrown into the Tiber River. The festival of Vesta was called Vestalia and was celebrated from June 7 to June 15.

Hestia's perpetual fire burned in every Greek City.
Image by Christian Baitg/Image Bank/Getty Images

Another deity associated with fire was Irish Brigit. Brigit was a smith, poet, and healer. Not coincidentally all her attributes were associated with fire. Healing power is very often associated with fire, just as blacksmithing, of course. The same is true of poetry which is often symbolized by the flame of inspiration. Brigit was another goddess of home and hearth and was worshipped as a Goddess and later as a Saint. She again was associated with the sacred flame. She had 19 priestesses and later nuns who tended her sacred flame for 19 days. On the 20th day, the fire was left unattended but still lit and people believed that the goddess herself was tending her flame on that day.

In myths, fire is associated with dragons and phoenixes. The Phoenix was a bird that lived for 500 years and then died in flames. After its death, it would be reborn out of the ashes. This myth relates to the idea of rebirth and renewal. It represents the ability of the human spirit to rise above adversity and persevere in the face of death.

△ Fire Correspondentes

Fire (Astrological rulers: Sun, Mars, Jupiter)

ZODIAC SIGN	Aries	Leo	Sagittarius
QUALITY	Cardinal	Fixed	Mutable
ELEMENT	Fire of Fire	Air of Fire	Water of Fire
ENERGY	Lightning	Sun	Rainbow
MANIFESTATION	Swift violence of onset	Steady force of energy	Fading spiritualized reflection of the image

Rules: Illuminative change and passion, light energy, sexuality, authority, purification, sun, blood, destruction, creativity, courage, strength, physical exercise, self-knowledge, power

Qualities: Hot, dry; light, active
Feminine Aspects: Mistress
Goddesses: Brigit, Hestia, Vesta, Freya
Gods: Vulcan, Ra, Agni, Horus
Direction: South
Hour: Noon
Season: Summer
Colours: Red, Orange, gold, crimson, brilliance
Weapons: Wand, Rod
Animals: Dragon, Lion, Phoenix
King of the elements : Djin
Angel: Aral
Ruler: Seraph
Spirits: Salamanders
Demon King: Paimon
Sense: Sight
Nature: Sun, stars, volcanoes, comets
Key Concept: Light
Part of the Soul: Chiah
Virtues: Passion, vitality, courage
Vices: Ruthlessness, greed, vengefulness
World: Atziluth - Emanation
Secret name of the Four Worlds: Aub
Emotion: Intensity
Magick: Healing (diseases), candle, storm, sun magic, cleansing

Imaginarium |43

Mythology

CIRCE_John_Collier_1885_-_Ger_Eatidti_Collection_The_NetherlandsFXD

SPRING IS
when Moly blooms

by Evangelia Papanikou

Moly: From the greek word "molos" meaning "hard" commemorating the harsh combat with Giant Picolous

Homer Odyssey, book 10, (lines 286-310 & lines 316-329) i

"But come, I will free thee from harm, and save thee. Here, take this potent herb, and go to the house of Circe, and it shall ward off from thy head the evil day. And I will tell thee all the baneful wiles of Circe. [290] She will mix thee a potion, and cast drugs into the food; but even so she shall not be able to bewitch thee, for the potent herb that I shall give thee will not suffer it. And I will tell thee all. When Circe shall smite thee with her long wand, then do thou draw thy sharp sword from beside thy

Imaginarium |44

Hermes giving the Moly to Odysseus

thigh, [295] and rush upon Circe, as though thou wouldst slay her. And she will be seized with fear, and will bid thee lie with her. Then do not thou thereafter refuse the couch of the goddess, that she may set free thy comrades, and give entertainment to thee. But bid her swear a great oath by the blessed gods, [300] that she will not plot against thee any fresh mischief to thy hurt, lest when she has thee stripped she may render thee a weakling and unmanned.' "So saying, Argeiphontes gave me the herb, drawing it from the ground, and showed me its nature. At the root it was black, but its flower was like milk. [305] Moly the gods call it, and it is hard for mortal men to dig; but with the gods all things are possible. Hermes then departed to high Olympus through the wooded isle, and I went my way to the house of Circe, and many things did my heart darkly ponder as I went."
[...]

iHomer. The Odyssey with an English Translation by A.T. Murray, PH.D. in two volumes. Cambridge, MA., Harvard University Press; London, William Heinemann, Ltd. 1919.

"And she prepared me a potion in a golden cup, that I might drink, and put therein a drug, with evil purpose in her heart. But when she had given it me, and I had drunk it off, yet was not bewitched, she smote me with her wand, and spoke, and addressed me: [320] 'Begone now to the sty, and lie with the rest of thy comrades.' "So she spoke, but I, drawing my sharp sword from beside my thigh, rushed upon Circe, as though I would slay her. But she, with a loud cry, ran beneath, and clasped my knees, and with wailing she spoke to me winged words: [325] "'Who art thou among men, and from whence? Where is thy city, and where thy parents? Amazement holds me that thou hast drunk this charm and wast in no wise bewitched. For no man else soever hath withstood this charm, when once he has drunk it, and it has passed the barrier of his teeth.'"

Shortly before Odysseus met sorceress Circe, while searching for his crew members -who had already gone ahead to explore Aeaea, Circe's island, and were transformed into animals under Circe's powerful spells - Hermes, the protector of travelers, gave Odysseus the antidote to the sorceress' potions and magic. It was the mythical herb Moly which grew from the blood of the giant Picolous who was killed on Aeaea by Helios, the sun god of Greek mythology and father and ally of Circe, when Picolous tried to attack his daughter.

Hermes advised Odysseus to eat and drink anything Circe would offer him without the fear of

Imaginarium |45

being bewitched and put in a state that he would be unable to react. Being alert, under the protection of Moly, Odysseus would be able to face Circe and threaten her immediately with his drown sword as soon as she tried to touch him with her magic wand and transform him too, to an animal. When his sword was drown and she was under him, she recognized him as the hero prophesied to her. She was the one enchanted instead of enchanting him. She begged him for her life and offered him her love. Odysseus accepted.

Known well for her powerful witchcraft, Circe embodies the magic force of nature. She grew more herbs and shrubs with medicinal properties: mandrake to protect herself, peony to ease pain, snowdrop and yarrow, poppy and rue. Moly, however was the most valuable and rare herb on her land, however one she probably did not have access to anytime she wished for either.

Moly achieved its magical purpose, having Odysseus enjoy his mortal life and opening the path to immortality for him. Maybe, Hermes "forgot" to mention one little thing to Odysseus, however:

whoever consumes Aeaean Moly, may enjoy many more divine benefits than just not being bewitched – among them the love and devotion of a mysterious sorceress goddess, knowledge and wisdom of safe havens, such as Ithaca's, valuable details of Poseidon's plans with him, safe passage to the underworld, even a form of immortality eventually - but as with all magical rituals, in return he is bound to the island of Aeaea and its owner.

Moly, as described by Homer, is a plant with roots of the colour of the night, same as the colour of the blood of giant Picolous, black. Its flowers have the colour of absolute light, either personifying bright Helios who killed the giant, or the fact that Circe grew pale of terror during Picolous' attack, pure white.

Moly, besides its magic properties, has one more strange characteristic by nature: only gods can pick it from the earth, a fact that makes its potential usage by mortals even more rare and special, such as that the only one reference of a common mortal using it being the one by Odysseus at Aeaea.

Edward_Burne-Jones_-_The_Wine_of_Circe,_1900

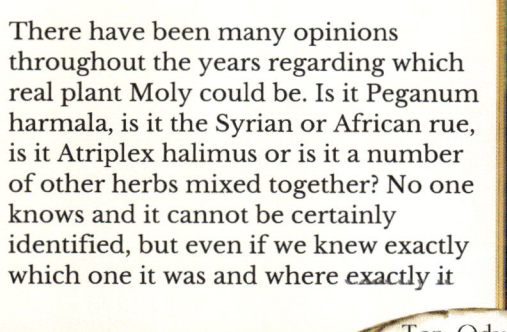

There have been many opinions throughout the years regarding which real plant Moly could be. Is it Peganum harmala, is it the Syrian or African rue, is it Atriplex halimus or is it a number of other herbs mixed together? No one knows and it cannot be certainly identified, but even if we knew exactly which one it was and where *exactly* it

*Top: Odysseus and Circe, Ponte Vecchio, Florence
Bottom: Odysseus and Circe, 1786*

Moly, along with the Prometheion, the special magical plant Medea used for her potions -which originated and grew from the blood of Prometheus- and Kirkaion or "Circe's plant" -an analogue to Moly, a type of toxic lily with magical properties Circe only knew how to use, available for her to pick and, for better or worse, anytime she wished- are the three mysterious herbs of magical Spring. What a better spring quest than locating all three of them!

Right: Homer (seated) and Hermes with the immolum (Moly). Allegory from a miniature from the Codex Medicina Antiqua, (fol. 61 verso)

grew and bloomed no human could actually pick it from the earth and use it, unless it was handed in to him/her by a god or goddess.

Besides Circe, her niece Medea and her sister Pasiphae and last but not least, the great sorceress goddess, Hecate are ancient Greek witches associated with herbal magic, potions and ointments.

John_William_Waterhouse_ Circe_Invidiosa_1892

Imaginarium |47

Photography

Model: Jackie Wyers

Imaginarium |48

Welcome to
LOST LANDS COLECTIONS
By Marianne Bell

We stepped into the ethereal world of Lost Lands Collections and we got to know all about the magical lenses of Marianne Bell.

Interview to Anastasia Diakidi

A. Hello Marianne, thank you so much for being here. We are so happy to welcome you and your work into Imaginarium World. Please tell us a few words about you and how your journey into photography began.

M. I have always had a deep appreciation and interest in many art forms. From a young age, I would draw and paint primarily, but it wasn't until college that I began to really dive into photography. At the time, I was also taking sculpting classes. I found that I loved creating all aspects of my images. I started making props and wardrobe and collecting items to create my magical worlds.

A. How would you define your art? What are the main elements of your art?

M. I use a lot of classical art for inspiration in my posing and editing. My work is very ethereal, and whimsical. I work with varieties of haze, and lighting, to add a dream-like vintage film feel. I lean toward light-flowing fabrics and texture—for wardrobe paired with a corset or prop—with fluid lines. I like everything to flow together!

A. It is obvious that legends and tales also inspire you. Would you like to tell us more about your inspirations? What inspires you to create a Lost Land moment?

M. Lost Lands Collections was born from my desire to escape. I grew up with extreme social anxiety, and later on, struggled with PTSD—my work has been a beautiful form of therapy and escapism.
When I was young I would watch any sort of fairytale film, or period drama/romance, and daydream endlessly of my own stories.

A. It is true, that art is a refuge to all of us who deal with such anxieties and I am happy you found such an amazing outlet. Not

only for you personally but because you also create something magical for the world and we have the pleasure to escape with you. Do you create your own projects or do you work with clients? Do you have specific models you work with as a team?

M. I do love to work with some of my close friends as models for special projects. But, when I'm not working on passion projects I'm working primarily with clients. No prior modeling experience is necessary, and I coach you through posing to help everything feel effortless. You can come to me with the beginning of an idea and I'll build off of that. I usually have colors or key pieces of wardrobe in mind after only a few ideas, and build a mood board from there.

A. Oh wow! Sounds amazing! And do you sell your prints? Where can we find them?

M. Yes, I do! I sell them on my website (*www.lostlandscollectionsllc.com*); I hope to showcase my work in a gallery this year!

A. Fantastic! We really hope you move on with such an endeavour and we wish you the best of luck! Also, I see on your website that you organize retreats around the world, please tell us more. Sounds very interesting. Are you involved in cosplaying? What do you do?

M. Yes, I love to travel and find fairytale locations to share! I do photograph cosplay, and LARP looks, for clients! I recently did a fun Avatar shoot, and a Galadriel look for Amazon Prime.

A. Exciting! Where do you find magic in real life?

M. I find magic in simple things– toads and bugs chirping in the distance.

A. How would you define beauty in our times? Especially nowadays that everything is digitally 'touched'.

Pages 49-51
Models: Gabi Demartino & Collin Vogt
Gabi's dress: French Meadows Corsets
Styling: Marianne Bell

M. My definition of beauty has always been a bit different than what's popular. I've always enjoyed very natural looks, but I love to challenge myself with new things and grow as an artist; I'm exploring with some 3D designers and sculptures on some futuristic fantasy projects.

A. How much work is it to take one photograph? It must be really hard work! How long does it take you to create the magical moment? Do you have assistants on the field or do you work alone?

M. It depends on the project, but I always put a great deal of energy into every idea. I really enjoy doing huge productions, with designers, and hair and makeup. Sometimes I hire an assistant or friend to travel with me most of the time. It's so much fun to load up my car with a bunch of random props and wardrobe, and just have fun with friends at some random spot we find.

A. Indeed. That's the best way and the more fun. What are your plans for the rest of the year and where could we find you?

M. I have several trips coming up for the spring and summer: SoCal, Washington, the UK, and my hometown in Connecticut! I love traveling to new places, and seeing what the world has to offer for new inspiration.

While in the UK, I'll be hosting a retreat in Wales, with a wonderful group of ladies from the UK, and a day event at an amazing castle. Anyone is welcome to participate, and you're more than welcome to join us when we arrive!

A. Thank you so much. We would love that and we are really looking forward to it. I wish you all the best in all your future endeavours and thank you for sharing space and your work with us.

Model: Sarita
Corset: French Meadows Corsets
Pillowcase: Artem Luxe
Styling: Marianne Bell

Find out more about Marianne and her work on
Instagram @lostlandscollections & beacons.ai/lostlandscollections

Imaginarium |52

Model: Sarita
Corset: French Meadows Corsets
Pillowcase: Artem Luxe
Styling: Marianne Bell

Imaginarium |53

Beauty & Wellbeing

The Witch's Cabinet

Beauty and Wellbeing with the Guidance of the Moon

All the planetary aspects the Moon forms are calculated for 9a.m UTC.

By Lucinda

Dear magical friends,

The month of April begins with the Moon in the sign of Leo and during the day it will meet Jupiter. Take advantage of the nice weather and Jupiter's beautiful meeting with the Moon and take walks outdoors, but don't limit yourself to that. Treat yourself to a few moments of relaxation with "smile breathing", which you can also apply anytime you feel stress or physical pain.

Sit somewhere quiet, find a quiet breathing rhythm, and just... smile. It may seem strange at first but keep at it. Feel yourself breathing through your nose and through your smile at the same time, and mentally direct the combined energy of breathing and smiling to the area of the body that feels tight or sore. Exhale through the mouth, relax, with a light breath, as if blowing out a candle, and imagine that the tightness or pain goes away. Continue for at least 5 minutes.

On April 3, the Moon moves into Virgo and it's a good time to begin a good internal cleansing.

The liver is the organ of the body associated with spring and the element of Wood. Now is the time to rid the body of toxins that have accumulated over the winter. If you are not vegan, at least reduce the fat in meats and dairy. For a good liver detox try drinking herbal drinks that have such properties, such as:

Fennel: Make an infusion of 5 grams of seeds in 1 glass of boiling water and strain after 10 minutes. Drink once a day.

Dandelion or taraxacum: Boil the root and drink one cup of tea twice a day.

Calendula: Add 10 gr of flowers and leaves to 3 glasses of hot water along with some rosemary. Strain after 10 minutes and drink them, one in the morning fasting and one half an hour before lunch and dinner.

Thyme & Rosemary: Make an infusion of 8 gr. in 2 glasses of hot water and drink one after lunch and dinner.

Agrimony: Add 5 gr of flowers and leaves to 2 glasses of hot water, leave for 10 minutes, strain, and drink one in the morning on an empty stomach and the other before going to bed at night.

Nettle: Drink an infusion of its leaves 3 times a day.

On April 6 we have the Libra Full Moon with the participation of Jupiter. What a great time to work on the issues of companionship and joy in your life! Decorate your space with objects that promote the energy of togetherness. For example, put touches of pink and red in your space - objects, fabrics, candles. Moreover, symbols of love, such as hearts, the winged god, rings, peonies, butterflies, and double objects - ducks, swans, and plants in the same pot. And even, pictures of your wedding or paintings and sculptures of embracing couples are good to have in your space to

Imaginarium |54

Photo Canva database

create vibrations of a happy companionship.

While on April 7 and 8 with Moon in Scorpio, it is good to work on libido and sexuality issues. Boost your libido and lift your mood by drinking a ginseng decoction.

Put a small root in boiling water and leave it for 15 minutes. Remove the root and sweeten the sprinkle with honey or add ginger and lemon if you like.

However if you have a decreased sex drive, *add 5 drops of ylang-ylang and sage essential oils to your bath or bedroom humidifier to enhance relaxation and increase your sexuality.*

On April 9 Christians celebrate Easter and Pagans celebrate Ostara, a spring fertility festival. Eggs are a favourite symbol of the celebration either on a Pagan or Christian level. On an astrological and symbolic level, the **Moon in the morning hours is moving at the last degrees of Scorpio**, a sign associated with death and rebirth, just before it passes into Sagittarius, a fiery sign of adventure and joy. On Easter Day or the day before you can decorate your eggs. In Eastern European countries there is a long tradition of dyeing eggs (done on the Thursday before Easter).

Although there are chemical dyes, if you are in favour of natural dyes for your Easter eggs, various kinds of edibles can provide you with all the colour tones you would like. For blue, you can use red cabbage leaves; for beige or brown strong coffee and black tea; for orange-brown chilli powder; for green spinach; for yellow carrots, cumin, saffron, turmeric, and yellow onion skins; for pink and red use beetroot, red onions or cranberries, cherry syrup or grape juice.

You will need white eggs, which you will have washed well and hard-boiled. Depending on how dark you want the color, put one to three handfuls of your ingredients in water (at least a cup of water for each handful), bring to a boil, and lower the heat to simmer for 15 minutes to an hour, again depending on the desired tone. Then strain the liquid, pour it into a large bowl, and add 2-3 tablespoons of white vinegar for each cup. Put in enough eggs to cover them with your paint, and leave them overnight, When you have the desired color, remove them with a slotted spoon, and let them dry on a rack or on their carton. Finally, polish them with olive oil.

Over the next two days, April 10 and 11 with the Moon in Sagittarius, plan activities that lift your spirits and boost your confidence. Go out with friends, take a sport, or enjoy nature.

On April 12 and 13, with the Moon in Capricorn, place a black tourmaline near the entrance of your home to prevent negative energy from entering, and a kunzite near the area where you spend long hours to ward off negative emotions and fears. An agate, to boost your morale, a topaz, against the dark forces, and an amber, to keep you from being touched by envy.

If you have melancholy and negative thoughts overwhelm you, essential oils: basil, geranium, tangerine, jasmine, and patchouli can help you. Pour two drops into the essential oil burner and inhale deeply.

On April 16 and 17, the Moon will be in Pisces and it is a good time to treat your feet. You're about to start wearing sandals, so it's time to pamper your feet that have been worn down by closed shoes.

Give your feet a good massage with almond oil, to which you will have added 1-2 drops of lemon or peppermint essential oil. Rub in circular motions on the foot and also the sole, using your thumb. Then, making a fist, knead the foot with your knuckles. Finish by gently rubbing the toes one by one. Once a week, before bedtime, apply a rich layer of hand cream to the feet and sleep in cotton socks. In the morning your feet will be velvety smooth!

On April 20 we have the Solar Eclipse in the sign of Aries and in conjunction with Pluto. The Eclipse speaks of closures in cycles that no longer have a future. This Eclipse is the first of the year and there will be three more to follow. Although its energy lasts not just one day but months, if you have heavy energy on this day, give your body and mind the gift of silence and tranquillity.

If the plutonic energy creates anxiety and phobias, burn essential oils that will calm you down.

- *4 drops of bergamot*
- *2 drops of tangerine,*
- *2 drops of geranium
 or alternatively*
- *1 drop of orange blossom*
- *3 drops of tangerine,*
- *2 drops of geranium*

On April 21, the Moon is in Taurus a beautiful placement for the Moon, and in the morning it conjuncts Mercury, which is stationary to turn retrograde.

Mercury's station and the Taurus sign can highlight issues with the throat area or voice.

Spring often brings many colds that pass quickly (and are useful as they detox the body!), but can leave the unpleasant persistent cough.

Try warding it off by boosting your body's defences with a simple visualization.

- Sit comfortably, close your eyes, and imagine for a

Imaginarium |56

few minutes that you are in a beautiful place that is calming you down.

- Take ten deep, slow, and quiet breaths. Concentrate on the feeling of the air as it passes through your throat.

- Imagine the inside of your throat as a tunnel. Normally its walls are smooth, but now they are filled with sharp pebbles.

- Visualize a golden light wrapping around your neck like a scarf. The light slowly penetrates its interior.

- The golden light spreads throughout your neck and melts the pebbles as if they were ice cubes. After a while, they are all gone and the inner walls of your neck are smooth.

- The golden light comes back out and stays for a while around your neck like a scarf. And as it fades, you slowly open your eyes.

Do this exercise daily in combination with your medical treatment until the discomfort is gone.

On April 23, with the Moon in Gemini and in conjunction with Venus, say...I love you! A good time to express your love to your loved ones.

On the 25th and 26th with Moon in Cancer, it's a great time to take care of family matters as well as do household chores. And since the Moon is in waxing, you can make positive and beneficial additions to the diet of the whole family.

On April 28 with Moon in Leo, you can treat your hair.

To give vitality, shine, and softness to dry hair, do the following:

Heat 100 ml of coconut oil in bain marie, add 100 ml of sunflower oil, and stir. Remove the mixture from the heat and add 10 drops of orange essential oil, 5 drops of geranium essential oil, and 5 drops of lavender essential oil. Stir and place the mixture in a dark glass bottle where it can be stored for about 6 months at room temperature.

Depending on the length of the hair, apply 1-3 tablespoons of this conditioner evenly to wet hair, from roots to ends. Massage for 1 minute, then wrap hair with a towel and leave on for about 30 minutes. Finish your treatment by shampooing with a neutral pH shampoo with natural ingredients.

On May 4 with Moon in Libra in trine aspect to Venus, take care of your body and feel beautiful!

A very... delicious recipe, which you can also make fatigue signs disappear from your skin. It cleanses the face, smooths and nourishes the skin, and is very easy to take with you on your travels.

All you need is *100 grams of almonds with their peel and 3 teaspoons of acacia honey. Finely chop the almonds and put them in a cup with the honey, forming a soft and elastic ball. Store the mixture in a closed container or plastic bag. Store in the refrigerator for 3 months and for 1 month at room temperature. If you want to give your masque also relaxing properties, add 5-6 drops of essential oil ylang ylang.*

How to use: Put a quantity of the mixture equal to the size of a hazelnut in your palm and mix it with a little water, forming a creamy emulsion that you apply to a clean face while gently massaging. Leave this moisturising, protective, and soothing mask on for 10 minutes, and then remove it with lukewarm water.

On May 5 we have a difficult Lunar Eclipse in Scorpio. If you need relief from a nervous headache:

- *30 ml of almond oil*
- *4 drops of peppermint essential oil*
- *6 drops of lemon essential oil*
- *6 drops of lavender essential oil*
- *1 drop of geranium essential oil*

In a dark brown bottle, mix the oil with the essential oils and shake well. Massage the temples, forehead, and around the ears.

Alternatively, if you need a mental boost:

- *1 drop of jasmine essential oil*
- *2 drops of lime essential oil*
- *2 drops of petitgrain essential oil*

Add the essential oils together with some water to the essential oil burner.

On May 7 and 8 with Moon in Sagittarius after a difficult eclipse, you may need extra fire energy! Wear coloured clothing preferably red and orange, or white. Also, consume red or orange foods.

The citrus family prides itself for the famous and precious vitamin C. The vitamin that, as we know, strengthens the immune system and preventively, aids against all kinds of illness and weakness. Citrus fruits are energizing fruits, but not only for the body. The healing properties of vitamin C extend to the psychological traumas of loss, separation, and bereavement.

Imaginarium |57

Orange will help you regain your self-confidence and inner strength, but without having to make compromises. In addition, it soothes anxiety attacks.

Tangerine is suitable for anyone who feels that they will not have love and approval in their life, even if they find themselves facing a crowd of thousands of people cheering them on.

Lemon is the perfect remedy for the pain caused by an emotional loss.

On May 12 with the Moon in Aquarius in an unfavorable aspect to Uranus and the Sun, you may experience increased nervousness.

This smooth, creamy, and soothing banana shake will help calm your mind. Rich in starch and nutrients thanks to the bananas, with their mild soothing properties, this sweet concoction is just what you need to combat your nervousness, especially if it comes from overwork and stress.

Ingredients for 1 serving:
- *250 ml of milk*
- *1 banana peeled and chopped*
- *4 ice cubes*
- *1 tbsp. honey*
- *1 pinch of nutmeg*
  If desired, serve with additional nutmeg.

On May 14 with the Moon in Pisces to have a relaxing sleep make a sleep pouch.

In a cloth pouch put 60 gr of chamomile, 30 gr of rosemary, and 15 gr of cloves. Place it inside your pillow and gently squeeze it to release its fragrance.

On May 19 we have a New Moon in Taurus in a favorable sextile to Mars and Neptune. This is an excellent time to work on your wishes and their fulfillment.

You can make a magic wish box.

Start by specifying what it is that you want. It may be about you being hired in a good position, the development of an acquaintance, or a happy outcome in a legal or financial matter. Make only one wish at a time, phrasing it clearly and asking, of course, for something achievable.

Wishes should be positive to exclude the possibility of harm to someone else.

No one should read them once they are in the box.

Put the paper with the wish in the box, reading it aloud three times without others hearing you.

After putting your wish in the box push the thought of your wishes to the back of your mind and start by taking simple practical steps to achieve what you dream of.

Use the method at most once a month and in the following weeks seek to offer to someone who hasn't treated you so well in the past. The following month you can put another wish in the box.

When the box is full; tie the wish cards with a red string, tie three knots, and bury the ashes under a fruit tree. Burning the wishes is a traditional way to release their energy into the universe. It is a symbolic gesture that activates your own powers so that whatever you wish comes true.

With the wish box, our wishes are symbolically formed and our handling of them becomes more direct. By leaving your wishes in a box without rereading them, you create space for your unconscious mind to devise ways to make them real. Then, when you release the wishes by burning them, you symbolically generate enough energy to activate them and make them bear fruit.

Have a lovely magical time and a blessed Spring!

Lucinda

Photo Canva database

Imaginarium |59

PLANETARIUM
The Diary of Planetary Influences

by Anastasia Diakidi

The dates given are when the aspects become exact. However, they start with their influence 1-2 days before and -in some cases- last 1-2 days after the given date. The degrees given mean that those who have planets or Ascendant/Midheaven on those degrees are influenced by the aspect. To get a copy of your natal chart check astro.com or email imaginarium.magazine.13@gmail.com

Cardinal Signs: Aries, Cancer, Libra, Capricorn
Fixed Signs: Taurus, Leo, Scorpio, Aquarius
Mutable Signs: Gemini, Virgo, Sagittarius, Pisces

A sign is 30° and it consists of 3 decans. A decan is the equivalent of 10 days, as a sign corresponds to 30 days. Those born on the 1st decan are born on the first 10 days (0-9°) of their sign, on the 2nd the following 10 days (10-19°) and those on the 3rd decan are born on the last 10 days (20-29°) of their sign.

3/4 Mercury Enters Taurus: The mind is becoming slower and preoccupied with ideas related to money, security, possessions, and beauty. During Mercury's journey through Taurus, until 11/6, one might sort out financial loose ends. It is also possible people come more in contact with nature, do more gardening activities, and embrace slow living. Careful with jealousy, materialism, possessiveness, and stubbornness. This a good period to seek practical solutions and reflect on the idea of self-worth. The placement benefits mostly the Earth and Water Signs.

& Mercury squares Pluto: The aspect is a double-edged sword and it requires a lot of inner balance to cope with it. The mind is troubled and prone to paranoia and phobias. It could be helpful if someone needs to persuade someone to achieve something. Craftiness could be used for good or evil. Be extra careful with children and pets. A good day for psychoanalysis and therapy sessions. It affects the Fixed signs, born on the very first few days of their signs (0°-3°) as well as the Cardinal signs born on the last day of their sign (29°). The aspects affect those who have planets/Ascendant/Midheaven in the above signs and degrees.

5/4 Mercury sextile Saturn: Strategic thinking, concentration, and focus are the keywords of this beneficial aspect. A great one to organize your life, do mental work and research, or communicate seriously with others. It also promotes agreeable solitude and rational self-reflection. It affects positively Taurus, Pisces, Cancer, and Capricorn. Scorpios and Virgos can be prone to depression and need to balance this energy. Delays, and bad mood. Affects all those who have planets/Ascendant/Midheaven from 0-3° and were born at the beginning of the first decan of all the above signs.

6/4 Full Moon in Libra: Relationships and initiatives are illuminated dynamically yet harmoniously. Situations balance and opportunities for balancing existing relationships are given. There is a romantic disposition and a mood of leisure. Battles are won with diplomacy.

7/4 Venus sextile Neptune: A romantic day. Favours flirting and activities involving art and relaxation. A good day to enjoy the sea, music, or art. We may even give money to enjoy something relaxing. Affects those with planets, Ascendant/Midheaven in Taurus, Pisces, Capricorn, and Cancer from 23-28°.

8/4 Mercury sextile Mars: Determination, haste, sharp spirit. Fast thinking and rapid progress. An aspect that brings practical solutions and mental assertiveness. A good day to learn technical skills. It favours mostly those who have planets/Ascendant/Midheaven in the signs of Earth and Water, especially in the first decan (2-10°)

11/4 Venus enters Gemini: this Venus is more playful and curious and more interested in intellectual activities and sharing ideas. This is how our love life will be for the time that Venus remains in this sign. A time when communication is lighter and we have lots of ideas for making money. It activates the love life of the Air signs as well as the Mutable signs. The above signs will also have favour in financial matters.

Imaginarium |60

& Venus trines Pluto: a very sexual aspect as relationships deepen and healthy sexuality increases. Social contacts are more profound. Financial successes. The aspect is especially favourable for those with planets, Ascendant or Midheaven in Gemini, Aquarius, and Libra from 0-4°. Also, those born in an Earth sign in the last days of their sign.

& Sun Conjuncts Jupiter: A wonderful aspect as it bears gifts and promises growth. It is very good for business, travel, and education. Careful only with risks as we are very optimistic and confident. This conjunction will bring fortune to Cardinal and Fire signs (and those who have planets/Ascendant/ Midheaven in them), mostly from 18°-25°.

14/4 Venus squares Saturn: a difficult aspect for the emotional and financial issues of the Fixed signs. Loneliness, inhibitions, and also separations or crises in couples. Financial problems. A day when utility outweighs beauty. Beauty work done on this day aims at a more serious and classic look. The aspect mainly affects Mutable signs or those who have planets, Ascendant/ Midheaven in a Mutable sign from 0°-8°.

20/4 Solar Eclipse in Aries: This solar eclipse marks the end of an era and the beginning of a new one through totally transformative situations. Yet there is no lack of tension in everyday life. Be careful when commuting as there is excessive nervousness and irritability. A good time for technological and practical solutions to everyday issues.

& Sun squares Pluto: A difficult aspect that could lead to great accomplishments if it is not wasted in power struggles, competition, and drama. The survival instinct is strong, the same as the sexual drive. Be careful as unconscious behaviour might reveal underlying motivations. Read the body language and use your gut to understand people's intentions. Careful with jealousy, sexual tension, obsession, violence, and manipulation. Focuses on the inability to share and trust others. It affects the Fixed signs, especially those who are born or have planets/ Ascendant/Midheaven in the first degrees (0-4°). It also affects the Cardinal signs born on the very last days of their signs (28-29°).

21/4 Mercury stations to turn retrograde: Mercury stations to turn retrograde in Taurus. Until the 15/5 we are called to reassess finances, love affairs as well as our security and values. The Fixed signs (especially 5-15°) will be affected in the important areas of their lives. Do not buy a new car, book traveling, or start a commercial or educational activity. Contracts signed during this period might go under changes in their terms and conditions after the retrograde period. Good time to re-evaluate existing situations and not start anything new.

24/4 Mercury retrograde sextile Mars: Determination, haste, sharp spirit. Fast thinking and rapid progress. An aspect that brings practical solutions and mental assertiveness. A good day to re-learn technical skills or reassess the work we have done. It favours mostly those who have planets/Ascendant/Midheaven in the signs of Earth and Water, especially in the first decan (12-19°).

25/4 Sun sextile Saturn: Logic. Steady achievement. Success in overcoming obstacles. Good relations with the authorities. Stamina. Patience. Concentration and mental focus. Success in overcoming limitations. Good judgment. Favourable for the Water and Earth signs as well as those who have planets/ Ascendant/ Midheaven in those signs (especially from 1-8°).

29/4 Mars sextile Uranus: A good aspect that brings technical creativity and resolutions to problems that have been lingering for some time. The aspect symbolizes the desire to make things happen, to force changes. Revolutionary ideas and radical decisions will bring positive changes to the business. Individuality is accentuated. It affects mostly those who have planets in Cancer, Taurus, Pisces, Capricorn, and Virgo (14-22°).

1/5 Pluto stations to turn retrograde: Pluto stops to turn retrograde until October 12. During its retrograde, it will return to Capricorn where it will bring its final and catalytic changes to the political system and governments. Because Pluto is associated with financial power during his retrograde period we have events involving financial scandals, and tax, treasury, and public money issues are stirred up. On an individual level when retrograde it creates a tendency to focus on 'bad things' in both personal and public life. We close in on ourselves more for fear of getting hurt, and become over-analytical and not at all spontaneous; we will confront our deepest fears and subconscious, and our inner demons will be reflected in the behaviour of others towards us. This is an ideal time to work with our souls and bring to light issues that are rooted in the past and are keeping us from moving forward. Psychology, psychotherapy, and self-awareness groups are ways of getting in touch with the unconscious as we are very receptive and tend to look for the unseen part of ourselves. It particularly affects those born in the last days of the Cardinal signs or those with planets/ Ascendant/Midheaven in the final degrees (27-29°). It also affects those born in the first two days of the Fixed signs or those with planets/ Ascendant/Midheaven in the first degrees (0-1°).

3/5 Sun conjuncts Mercury: Mental strength that could benefit pioneering activities, business planning, and other activities related to personal promotion. Thought is intense and especially stimulated for writing, or speech. A good aspect for meeting up demands with courage and determination. Affects positively the Water the Earth signs, 8-15° or those who have planets/ Ascendant/ Midheaven. Although Scorpio, Aquarius, and Leo (8-15°) might have mental tension with this aspect. Be careful when driving.

4/5 Venus square Neptune: an aspect that needs caution in emotional matters as well as in professional and financial ones. Overimpressionability and weakness of judgment can lead to emotional as well as financial deceptions. Excessive sentimentality as well as romantic fantasy. The aspect can also give disappointments as well as defeatism in emotional issues. Care needs to be taken by those born in Mutable signs or who have planets, Ascendant/ Midheaven in them (24-29°).

5/5 Venus sextile Jupiter: a beautiful aspect for friendliness, generosity, and pleasant social contacts. Romantic encounters and financial agreements are favoured. A good day for big parties and beautiful appearances. The aspect positively affects Aries, Gemini, Aquarius, Leo, Libra, and Sagittarius and also those with planets, Ascendant/Midheaven in these signs, especially from 24 -29°.

& Lunar Eclipse in Scorpio: This lunar eclipse is extreme and explosively emotional. It may involve deception and betrayal. It brings revelations that require skill in managing the emotional tension they may cause. Tremendous passion and financial losses. It is especially difficult for the Fixed signs.

7/5 Venus enters Cancer: Venus in this sign becomes

sensitive and nurturing. Our love behaviour sweetens and we may become closer to our family. It favours income from real estate or family businesses. It energizes those with Venus and other planets in Cancer as well as the rest of the Water and Earth signs.

9/5 Sun conjuncts Uranus: This aspect may trigger an upheaval in the world but it may be beneficial on a personal level as it forces us to take action and get things done. The aspect has also a lot of nervous tension. Appliances and machinery may break down. The mind is inventive and the aspect might help us achieve something innovative, or progressive. A good day to join with others for a specific cause or purpose. Bear in mind that breakups and tension are also possible, especially for the Fixed Signs. The aspect is beneficial for Cancer, Virgo, Capricorn, and Pisces. It affects those born in the middle of the above signs (16-22°).

12/5 Mercury sextile Saturn: Strategic thinking, concentration, and focus are the keywords of this beneficial aspect. A great one to organize your life, do mental work and research, or communicate seriously with others. It also promotes agreeable solitude and rational self-reflection. Favourable for the Water and Earth signs as well as those who have planets/ Ascendant/ Midheaven in those signs (2-10°).

13/5 Mercury sextile Venus: This aspect signifies the spirit of compromise. A good day to bridge the communication gaps with others and achieve harmonious interactions. Favourable aspect for intimate relationships as well as business agreements. There is clarity and flow in social conversations. A good day to appreciate beauty. Favourable for the Water and Earth signs as well as those who have planets/ Ascendant/ Midheaven in those signs (2-10°).

& Venus trines Saturn: a positive aspect as it stabilizes relationships and finances. Good for financial business deals. Diplomacy, duty, loyalty, economy, and good judgment are some of the good things about this aspect. It affects Water and Earth signs and those with planets, Ascendant/Midheaven in them (2-10°).

15/5 Mars trine Neptune: A creative aspect that brings the willingness to take action based on faith. Ideological success or desire for adventure and risk. Demonstration of strong emotions. Affects the Water signs from 24-29 °.

& Mercury turns direct: communication starts to flow better. Paperwork or study and travel issues are unblocked if there were any delays during the retrograde period. Issues that were reviewed are now put in place. The Fixed signs will be relieved.

16/5 Jupiter enters Taurus: The planet of expansion enters Taurus where it will bring luck, opportunity, and expansion to the Earth and secondarily the Water signs. Leos, Scorpio, and Aquarius will also benefit from it, but restraint will be needed as over-optimism and increased self-confidence can lead to wrong decisions. Studies, travel, foreign affairs, and legal matters are favoured for all the above signs. Jupiter will remain in Taurus until May 2024. This placement favours our financial and emotional security.

18/5 Jupiter squares Pluto: Perhaps the most important aspect of the year. Ambitious mood and awakening of your desires. Resistance however from others brings internal and external struggle and misunderstandings. Improvement work, restoration, or rebuilding of damage or harm. Reorganization or reform of a business, institution, or political system. Need for compromise on issues that you see most people agree on. Not a good time to make purchases. In religious or metaphysical interests carefully reconsider your views. In legal matters, you may not find the solutions or access you need, but under no circumstances accept illegal agreements. Connections with underworld people under this transit are very likely to bring conflict with the authorities. On a social level, the aspect can create further financial crises. It affects signs of the Fixed Cross born in the first three days of these signs as well as those who have planets/Ascendant/Midheaven in them (0-3°). Also, those born in a Cardinal sign (born in the last 2-3 days of these signs) or who have planets/Ascendant or Midheaven in them (28-29°).

& Sun sextile Neptune: A beneficial aspect that brings inspiration, creativity, and a need for giving or spirituality. It favours Water and Earth signs, especially from 24-29°. Also, those who have planets, Ascendant, or Midheaven in the above signs and degrees.

19/5 New Moon in Taurus: This New Moon brings the realization of goals and high capacity for organization. Be careful not to tread on dead bodies in the realization of goals. Unusual success and great reserves of energy.

& Mercury sextile Saturn: Strategic thinking, concentration, and focus are the keywords of this beneficial aspect. A great one to organize your life, do mental work and research, or communicate seriously with others. It also promotes agreeable solitude and rational self-reflection. Favourable for the Water and Earth signs as well as those who have planets/ Ascendant/ Midheaven in those signs (2-10°).

20/5 Mars enters Leo: Vitality and fighting spirit are strong in everything we do and we set high goals that we try to achieve. With Mars in Leo, we make a vibrant impression and have an influential presence and great confidence. Careful not to become demanding of others or arrogant. Dramatic expression. Generosity and amorous enthusiasm, playful attitude, and warmth. Mainly affects the determination and sexual life of the Fire signs. Scorpio, Aquarius, and Taurus might experience tension (also sexual) and irritability.

21/5 Mars opposition Pluto: an aspect that produces a lot of energy that is often spent on the urge for dominance. It gives intense sexuality but violence and obsession need to be considered. The aspect can be helpful in attempting personal transformation or in achieving a very difficult goal, even a physical task. Strategy but also the need to control the other person. The aspect affects those born in a Fixed sign or who have planets, Ascendant or Midheaven in them (0-4°) as well as those born in a Cardinal sign or who have planets, Ascendant or Midheaven in them (28-29°).

Imaginarium |62

& Sun trines Pluto: creative power, leadership skills, appreciation, and desire for psychological rebirth through unresolved situations. Stamina. Intuition and pragmatism in the business opportunities that appear. It is a great aspect for business. It affects the Air signs, especially those born in the very first days of their signs. Also, those who have other planets/ Ascendant/ Midheaven in the Air signs (0-4°) and Cardinal signs (28-29°).

22/5 Sun sextile Mars: The aspect favours physical exercise. Self-motivated action will resolve problems and make things happen. It favours initiative. Decisiveness leads to accomplishment. A good day to handle stress and start demanding activities. It affects mostly those who are born or have planets/Ascendant in Fire and Air signs (0/4°). Also affects those who have been born in the last few days of the Earth and Water signs (27-29°).

23/5 Mars square Jupiter: Success in business. Overcoming obstacles. Overexcitement and overconfidence. Lack of moderation. Inclinations to hasty actions and opinions. Competitive reactions. Lawsuits. It affects the Fixed signs and those with planets, Ascendant/Midheaven in them (0-5°).

26/5 Venus sextile Uranus: Exciting interaction with others, love at first sight, and rejuvenating new meetings are possible with this aspect. A day we could share an exciting activity with others and have fun doing something new. Affection might be expressed in unusual ways. Pleasant surprises. Creativity favours progressive styles. The aspect influences those who have planets or are born in Earth or Water signs (17-23°).

28/5 Sun square Saturn: An unpleasant aspect as it heralds trials and struggles. Problems, obstacles, limitations, inhibitions, and delays make it difficult to maintain control over our life. The feelings of insecurity may stimulate ambition and the desire to prove one's self-worth. The aspect is a burden for the Mutable Signs and those who have planets/ASC/MC on those signs, from 3-11°.

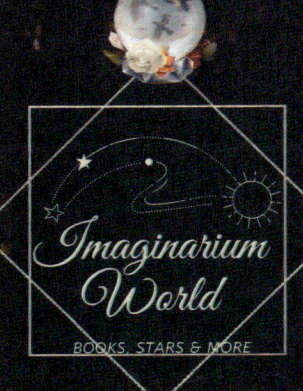

Discover your True Self

Enchant your Life

Join the Community

Imaginarium World
BOOKS, STARS & MORE

IMAGINARIUM MAGAZINE
Supper in Necromancton

HEKATE'S Supper
Gather Victoria

The Romantic Melancholy of NOM KINNEAR KING

MARIA LIPINA PHOTOGRAPHY
Early Vampiric Literature

THE DAY OF THE DEAD

GERMANY: Castle Frankenstein

An astromagical hub

ONLINE SHOP   MAGAZINES   ASTROLOGICAL SERVICES   COURSES   ONLINE EVENTS

https://imaginariumworld.co.uk
Email: imaginarium.magazine.13@gmail.com

Imaginarium |63

Astrology Lesson No 19

CUSPS & HOUSE OVERLAY II

As we explained in a previous issue the cusps are the boundaries of the houses, i.e. the dividing lines in the circle of our chart. The cusps are the most influential places in the house. We continue with the second part of this lesson, what it means when each house cusp corresponds to a zodiac sign.

By Anastasia Diakidi

Libra in the Angles

ASC (1st): Popularity and individuality projected through cooperation with others. Individuals express themselves with grace and beauty and there is a strong sense of justice. Ability to see things from others' point of view however you cannot be left alone and you make great compromises for this.

DES (7th): You are attracted to charming and kind people. Idealism and high romantic mood. Partners may have Libra, Venus, or Saturn traits and may also have a talent for public relations. They present a good image to the world.

MC (10th): People who attract attention because of their appearance and artistic ability. Often professions have Libra or Venus and Saturn elements, i.e. they are associated with beauty, artistry, fairness, and public relations. The desire for balance between family and professional goals. A partner may be found in the workplace. Strong sense of ethics in work matters and usually have a good reputation and standing in the community. Ability to win over people who have power and this can give them favour in promotions. The mother may have traits of Venus and Saturn or Libra, both in profession and character.

IC (4th): The house has elegance and beauty. There may be many tasteful art objects in the home to which you may also be emotionally attached. Justice to all members of the family otherwise problems are created which spoil the peaceful atmosphere of the home. A desire for harmony and tranquillity in the home but also a home that often hosts congenial people. The father may be fair, very handsome, or do some professions related to Libra, Venus, or even Saturn.

House cusps in Aries

2nd: You enjoy having money as this allows you to surround yourself and your space with beautiful things. With favorable aspects of Venus, it is likely that the person will not have financial problems in their life as they are always attracted to abundance. There may be financial ventures with a partner or spouse. There may be alternations between frugality and extravagance. Money may come from activities related to art, beauty, justice, and public relations.

3rd: Thoughts and ideas are expressed gracefully. There is a need for others to agree with you and the mind is generally very refined. There may have been flirtations or even the first serious relationship in adolescence and school years. Siblings may have Libra or Venus and Saturn qualities. A friendly relationship with siblings and neighbours. You like to travel in luxury and comfort. You may like to be surrounded by people who have nobility, beauty, and grace.

5th: Intense popularity. Tendency to an intense social life. Love life is volatile but characterized by romance.

Picture 2

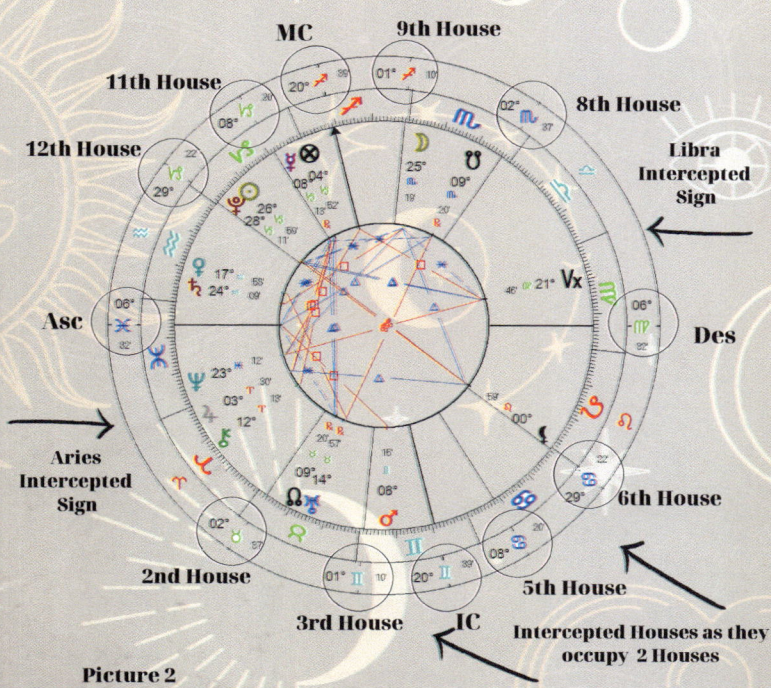

In your chart look the zodiac sign of each cusp -as it is circled in the picture- and read the equivalent overlay.
In this chart, the first angle corresponds to Pisces, the second house cusp corresponds to Taurus etc.

Partnerships are a channel for your creative power. You attract romantic partners who have grace and balance. Your hobbies may be related to music or the arts, and you yourself have artistic abilities of which you may not be aware. You enjoy intellectual conversations in your social circle.

6th: Libra, Venus, or Saturn-related professions. You seek harmony and a cooperative spirit with your colleagues and employees. You work effectively with others. You often seek partnerships that are however pleasant and harmonious. Health problems may be related to the kidneys.

8th: Ability to relate closely to others and appreciate what they have to offer. Strong sensitivity in relationships. Companions who contribute to shared finances. Benefits from inheritances and insurance. Cooperative spirit in methods that can bring in money. Sexuality is expressed with grace, sensuality, and elegance.

9th: Studies may be related to Venus, Saturn, or Libra themes, for example, studies in public relations, fine arts, law, etc. The philosophy of life is based on harmonious and beautiful coexistence with people. You like to travel for pleasure with your companions and dear friends. This placement may also indicate marriage in a foreign country or with a foreign partner. Spouses may have a good education and general education.

11th: You have a natural charm that attracts people around you but you need to be careful with whom you establish close relationships. Friendships last over time

and friends may have artistic interests. There is a possibility of marriage with a friend.

12th: Overly sensitive to the needs of others which often victimizes you. You may seek to isolate yourself in places of beauty and tranquility. Your hidden strength is your sense of fairness and fair play. Your weakness may come from your subconscious desire for luxury, and there may be narcissism. Be careful not to make intense compromises due to fear of loneliness.

Scorpio in the Angles

ASC (1st): You have a strong presence and your energy and will are projected powerfully into your environment. The look is strong and exudes intense sexuality. You have a steady yet powerful emotional intensity. You can achieve your goals at all costs. You have the ability to draw on hidden sources of power to attain your ends.

DES (7th): You are attracted to strong and reserved personalities. Partners may have Scorpio or Pluto qualities. You may need their help to feel passionate. Strong sexuality. Stable and fateful partners. Crises and rebirth through marriage. Attraction from status and power. Looking for energetic partners who have strong creative energy and the ability to succeed. Beware of the jealousy and possessiveness of your partners.

MC (10th): Professions associated with Scorpio or Pluto, such as psychotherapists, researchers, or anything to do with the occult and death. There may be some secrecy in matters of profession or public image in general. Career crises but also a tendency to rebirth even after a disaster. The mother has Scorpio or Pluto traits, such as being very controlling, and the relationship with her is fateful. There may also be a loss of her at a young age.

IC (4th): You have strong feelings about family for the home. You tend to keep your family affairs private and are extremely protective and loyal to your family. The house may be located in a disreputable neighborhood. The father may have Scorpio or Pluto qualities, there may be a fatal relationship with him or even the loss of him at a young age.

House cusps in Scorpio

2nd: You may be overly possessive of money and acquisitions. Your values may come through the acquisition of possessions and material success may give you confidence. You are very resourceful and energetic in the ways you make money. Ability to transform materials that have no value into something of real worth. Money may come from dealing with Scorpio or Pluto-related activities.

3rd: Having firm ideas and opinions in everything you learn and think about. You are very forceful in your mode of expression. Honesty that borders on bluntness. There may be a fateful relationship with siblings or they may have Scorpio or Pluto traits in their character and by extension their profession. The

Imaginarium |65

teenage years may also have been marked by a fateful incident.

5th: You tend to fall in love with those you are physically attracted to and this can often cause problems in sexual relationships as you may choose people who are not good for you. You may have fateful love affairs and also the loss of a romantic partner at some point in life. Your children may have intense emotionality. Be careful not to be possessive with your children and love partners. Extremely sensual in your romantic life. You may have hobbies that involve secret or occult pursuits. Your self-expression has emotional intensity.

6th: You can be a dedicated worker and try to do the best job possible. You are committed and serious about work. Professions may be associated with Scorpio or Pluto. Regeneration through service and work. Crises at work or with employees. You have success if you offer silently. Your health is affected by expressing or repressing your desires. If you repress your desires and also the sexual energy you may be led to health problems related to the genitals.

8th: Secrecy in matters relating to joint finances. You fight fiercely for what you need to acquire. You may have secrets as well as conflicts with matters concerning your joint finances with your partner. There may also be problems in matters concerning inheritances and wills. Financial empowerment through a will or inheritance. Powerful sexuality.

9th: Studies related to Scorpio or Pluto, for example, psychology, molecular sciences, forensics, etc. A crisis may have been created during the years of study that made education and completion difficult. Fateful connections with countries and people from abroad. You are passionate in expressing your personal philosophy but may be dogmatic in matters of faith. Metaphysical interests. Involvement with witchcraft.

11th: You are surrounded by dynamic yet strong individuals and your friendship with them stands the test of time. However, the relationship with them can often be life-changing. You rarely choose friends who are weak. Many of them also hold powerful positions and can be influential.

12th: You may be overly shy and retiring. However, it is possible that you may also be manipulative under the surface. Your hidden strength is your resourcefulness. You perceive what others have overlooked. You know how to activate the hidden talents of others. Your flaw and your downfall can be caused by secret resentment and hidden love affairs.

Sagittarius in the Angles

ASC: You present yourselves with optimism and dynamism. You are cheerful, you have large-scale goals. Your strength comes from your ability to influence other people positively. You are a source of optimism and inspiration to those around you.

DES: You are attracted to enthusiastic and popular types who have broad philosophical, religious, and moral backgrounds. They have values and innate wisdom. It can be an indication of more than one marriage, luck in partnerships, and many clients if you are a freelancer. Partners may have Sagittarius or Jupiter traits, both in physical characteristics and in character or profession.

MC (10th): You like to show off your intellectual skills. You may promise a lot that you can't deliver at work. It is an indication of many professions, career changes, and careers in areas related to the church, universities, publishing, foreign affairs, and travel. The mother may have Sagittarius or Jupiter qualities, meaning she is optimistic, and adventurous and may have instilled her values and philosophy of life in you. Her profession may be related to Sagittarius as well.

IC (4th): Your home may be large or you may have a large family. You open your home generously to your guests and are generally very generous to your own family as well. The family may have an academic or religious background. You usually get along well with them and are favored by your family. The father may have Sagittarius or Jupiter qualities in physical characteristics or even profession. He may also be from abroad.

House cusps in Sagittarius

2nd: You are very generous with your money and acquisitions but can often be wasteful because you are chasing the good life. Your money may come from Jupiter-related matters, such as having income from abroad. You generally have good luck in your financial matters and know how to make and multiply your money.

3rd: Your way of expressing yourself has natural optimism and exuberance. You have a natural talent for communication. The teenage years had adventures but also a lot of learning, and school may have been abroad or generally very long and prestigious. The relationship with siblings is usually very good and siblings may have Sagittarius or Jupiter qualities. The position may give frequent communication with foreign countries and people in faraway lands.

5th: You are very over-confident in your romantic life and are generally generous and good-natured. However, you don't like commitment and may not always be honest about your intentions. You have plenty of romantic adventures and may have love affairs with people from abroad. Your children are happy and they may also have some connection with overseas, religion or their profession may be related to universities or publishing. You like to provide the best for your children to the point that you may spoil them. You are very artistic and creative and enjoy large and lavish parties. Hobbies and activities include sports, religion, or philosophy.

6th: A placement that can show a lot of work and intense daily life. Good relationships with colleagues and employees with whom you can be a source of inspiration. May indicate professions related to Sagittarius or Jupiter. You like to give generously and inspire people to think and view life more positively. Health problems may stem from reckless drinking and eating, obesity, diabetes, or even liver problems. There may also be problems with the legs.

8th: You have favour in matters of joint finances. You may benefit from large-scale enterprises that grow and prosper. There may be intense financial activity in matters involving joint finances, insurance, inheritances, and loans. There may also be favour from inheritance. Your partners are usually financially stable. Liberating sexuality, without inhibitions.

9th: You have values and a philosophy of life that sees the positive side of the world. You like to philosophize. You love studying and traveling to foreign cultures and learning about people's cultures. Great interest in higher education, politics, and religion. It may indicate study abroad or studies in Sagittarius or Jupiter subjects, for example, political sciences, religious studies, tourism professions, and publishing.

11th: Your friends are optimistic and inspire you to greater accomplishments. You usually have many, many friends with whom you like to exchange ideas and discuss philosophical and political issues or engage in sports. Your friends may also come from abroad and you generally do not hesitate to have friendships with people from different backgrounds. You see the future with optimism.

12th: When you are alone you usually work through philosophical questions and try to find the meaning of life. Your self-undoing is that you have lofty aspirations which you cannot put into practice. You may have secrecy about some philosophical and religious beliefs.

Capricorn in the Angles

ASC: Discipline, hard work, and patience. Everything you do has a purpose and is designed to bring about practical results and success. Melancholy and serious nature, usually restrained.

DES: You are attracted to serious people who exude maturity. Partners are often very serious and have Capricorn or Saturnian traits. Marriages are long-lasting, especially if they are not done at a young age. Marriage for status. Cautious and reserved in establishing relationships. Difficulty in divorce. Problems with open enemies.

MC: Strong ambition and desire to achieve professional advancement through competition. You move slowly and methodically and always succeed. Indication for a career in Capricorn or Saturn professions such as management or architecture. Even though in the early years of life the career has a very slow rise and usually in the years of maturity you have a big boost. However, it is through hard work and great competition. The mother may have Capricorn or Saturn traits in character or even profession and the relationship with her may be very disciplined.

IC: There is great order and organization in the home. This may indicate deprivation in the home and family environment, especially at a young age. In the later years of life, you may seek solitude or seclusion. Dwellings in mountainous areas. Families that are strict and conservative and have rules for society's good opinion. Father has Capricorn/Saturn qualities in both character and profession. He can also be quite strict but also afflicted by the hardships of life.

House cusps in Capricorn

2nd: Practical, and responsible but with an ambitious attitude towards money and acquisitions. You don't spend recklessly or on a whim, you are generally very much a saver and buy things that have value in time. You may have income from Capricorn or Saturn-related sources. Life values have a more material background.

3rd: Your thinking is careful, as are your words. You never say anything unless you are sure of the reason for doing so. You may be intensely secretive and there may be a calculation or harsh criticism. The teenage years may have been deprived and generally difficult years and relationships with siblings may be difficult too. Siblings also have Capricorn or Saturn qualities in both characteristics and occupation.

5th: You are generally shy and reserved in sex and romantic relationships. You seem aloof and reserved. Yet as an earth sign, Capricorn is overly sexual. You are attracted to the maturity and prestige of a romantic partner. You don't like to gamble and generally take your pleasures too seriously or too calculatingly. You have high ambitions for your children with whom the relationship may have several difficulties. The children themselves may have Saturn or Capricorn traits in their personality or even in their profession.

6th: The placement indicates Saturnian professions such as management, architecture, or even tough professions that have hard work. Generally, it can be an indication of difficult karma at work. You are very serious about the services you offer and have professionalism and responsibility. You work hard and are very organized. There may be a difficult relationship with other employees. Work usually stands the test of time. Health problems may be related to bones, teeth, or skin.

8th: There may be a sexual blockage or even a complex in which there may be over-indulgence. Difficulties in matters relating to joint finances, loans, and inheritances. If you receive an inheritance there may be a delay in bureaucratic procedures and legal complications cannot be ruled out.

9th: The outlook on life has traditional and conservative foundations. You may follow religion dogmatically, and your philosophy of life may be based on somewhat more grounded and pragmatic concepts. You may of course be limited by materialism. There may be difficulty in completing studies, and there may be problems with long-distance travel and foreign cultures. Responsibility in matters relating to studies, publications, and travel. Studies in fields related to Capricorn or Saturn.

11th: Your friends are serious and responsible and may have Capricorn or Saturn traits in personality or profession. Your friends are stable but also somewhat conservative. Your hopes and the way you see the future is dominated by your desire for security.

12th: Inside you may be more conservative than you

Imaginarium |67

project to the world. You may be blocked by unconscious fears. Your hidden strength is the power of discipline. You work hard behind the scenes. You are good at keeping other people's secrets and generally work on secret projects.

Aquarius in the Angles

ASC: Independent and original spirit, wants to contribute to the common good. Friendly but in an impersonal way. You may find strength through your originality and eccentricity as well as your team and your social network or friends.

DES: You may be attracted to eccentric partners or one who is generally very independent and somewhat more emotionally detached. You also like to feel free and not tied down in a relationship. Partners have Aquarius, Uranus, or Saturn qualities.

MC: There is a tendency to work in teams and career-related matters there may be involvement in large corporation and group endeavours. Your career has stability however there may be eccentric elements; your profession may be unusual and innovative. Careers in professions related to Aquarius, Uranus, or Saturn, for example, technology, computers, robotics, new technologies, and also alternative professions such as astrology. The mother also has Aquarius, Uranus, or Saturn qualities in both character and profession. The relationship with her may have been friendly but also somewhat emotionally detached.

IC: Your home environment is unusual and distinctive. You may be staying with friends or generally hosting them in your home very often. There may be a detachment but also a distancing from family members, and you may consider your family to be your friends more than the people you have blood ties to. The father has Aquarian, Uranus, or Saturn qualities in occupation and/or character. The relationship with him may have been detached, overly friendly, or too cold.

House cusps in Aquarius

2nd: You may be making money in unusual, quite innovative ways which may be associated with organizations and also groups. You may be associated with corporate enterprises and produced the most ingenious techniques. Your life values and also security may come from your contribution to the common good.

3rd: The mind is innovative. Wit and mind-broadening. Your thinking and communication are lacking in sentimentality. The teenage years may have had some shocks as well as freezing relationships with people. Friends and groups were very important in the school years. The relationship with siblings may be detached and there may be a general lack of stability in the relationship, often there may be an alternation between detachment and friendliness with them. The siblings themselves may have Aquarius, Uranus, or Saturn characteristics.

5th: The placement may indicate love affairs with friends or unusual matches in general. As romantic partners, you are more detached and are sexually attracted to people who stimulate your mind. Pleasures come from unusual things but are also shared with friends and peers. Your children have wit and innovative nature and may have Aquarius, Uranus, or Saturn traits in their character.

6th: You are creative and innovative in the workplace. You are often involved with labour groups and unions. You generally have good and friendly relationships with your colleagues. You are methodical in your profession working in teams and using original techniques. You also want to offer service for the common good. To be successful in your work you must be eccentric and innovative and you must also work in a team. Health problems may be unusual or related to the neurological system.

8th: Sexuality is liberal and more connected to the intellect than the body. The placement may also indicate the ability to be psychic as you may have abilities with your mind in occult matters. The death of friends affects you deeply. In matters of shared finances, you have a team spirit. Wills or inheritances that may come to you may come suddenly but there may be shocking events associated with them.

9th: You have an original and unique view of the world. Your philosophy of life has no traditional structures. You may also generally not follow a traditional religion and may be more open to some New Age concepts for example. When travelling you like to get in touch with different cultures generally you may prefer travelling to unusual places. It is not excluded making friends abroad but generally, there may be shock involved in travelling. Studies are related to Aquarius, Uranus, or Saturn, for example, you may have studied astrology, technology, or some other New Science.

11th: You work very well with groups of people and generally have lots of friends. Your friends are usually diverse or even eccentric people. Your relationship with them may have some ups and downs, i.e. you may get disconnected and then reconnect. Friends may have Aquarius, Uranus, or Saturn characteristics. Your hopes and goals are always looking to the future and there may be unusual goals and visions for life.

12th: There may be an unconscious desire to serve humanity and you generally have a universal awareness that allows you to reach deeper levels of consciousness. You may have some extraordinary abilities, for example, telepathy, and may also receive inspiration from the Higher Mind. Your self-undoing may come from problems of alienation, especially from friends. They may of course be your hidden strength and support.

Pisces in the Angles

ASC: Sensitive to the subtle currents of your environment. Sympathetic and adaptable. You have a mystical approach to life that allows you to perceive human nature differently and more subtly. You can often sense the moods and auras of the people around you, which can be distracting. There is artistic and musical ability.

DES: You are attracted to partners who are highly sensitive, perhaps a little chaotic and weak. Your partners and associates may have Pisces, Neptune, or

Imaginarium |68

Jupiter characteristics. Through them, you enhance your emotional world and your understanding. The people you are attracted to are not as organized as you and you are often called upon to take on some of the practical aspects of daily life with them.

MC: Your profession has elements of Pisces, Neptune, or even Jupiter i.e. it may be related to artistic professions, religion, mysticism, or even charity. In general, you may have a blurred image of yourself in society. However, you are generally visionaries, though practically you may have problems at work. Your social reputation needs caution as it may suffer at some point in your life. There may be strange situations related to your reputation as well as your work, and there may be an element of mystery in your professional activity. The mother may be sensitive, have a strong connection with religion, the sea, and institutions, and may have some psychological problems. She may also have had some other Pisces, Neptune, or Jupiter traits in her character and profession.

IC: Your home is a place for a retreat where you leave the world aside and step into the space where you can relax and recharge your batteries. You may sometimes have your homes provided by large institutions, you may for example have residences provided by the university or live in ashrams. You value your privacy and your home is generally peaceful but there is a strong element of art or mysticism. The father may have Pisces, Neptune or Jupiter influences in his profession or even his character. That is, he may be very emotional, and physically sensitive, he may be generally lost/absent and there may be ambiguity and idealism about his presence, and his profession may be, for example, a pharmacist or related to the sea or chemistry.

House cusps in Pisces

2nd: Excessive generosity and lack of practicality in financial matters. According to the law of reciprocation, however, money may be lost but may never be lacking as your generosity may be returned to you in other ways by the universe. You are not greedy but appreciate the beautiful things in life. Your security comes from more mystical and more transcendent values. Money also may come from issues related to Pisces, Neptune, or even Jupiter.

3rd: There is a clouded mind yet very intuitive. Communication is more emotional and generally characterized by high EQ. You may feel the need to pull back to do mental work and just put your mind in order as you may tire more and easier mentally when you are with people. Your ideas are based on intuitive insights. Relationships with siblings and neighbours are quite emotional or even a bit...unconditional to the extreme. You may be inclined to give selflessly to them without stopping. Siblings also may have Pisces, Neptune, or Jupiter traits in personality or profession. The school years and teenage years may have had ambiguous situations in the environment and generally very high emotional tension.

5th: You are very romantic in love and serve those you love wholeheartedly without any selfishness and often with a great deal of self-sacrifice. Your hobbies are artistic and through them, you can escape from reality. There may be some mystery related to your children but your

6th: You may have delicate health and may have some sight problems or foot conditions. In general, you should be careful what medications you take as misdiagnoses may be made or you may have side effects from chemicals. Work may be related to chemistry, the sea, or other professions of Pisces, Neptune, and Jupiter. Work and service require unselfish devotion. You are sympathetic to employees and other employees. However, confusion and problems may arise in the workplace. The placement may also show hypochondriac tendencies. Health in general is related to your emotional state.

8th: There may be obscurities and secrets in matters related to joint finances with your partners, inheritances, wills, and loans. If you take out a loan beware of any collateral you put down. In general, there may be strange situations and losses. Sexuality has transcendence and it is through sex that you usually feel complete. Strong metaphysical concerns and pursuits.

9th: Your outlook on life has a mystical connotation. Religion can play a very important role in your life and if not in a dogmatic way, certainly in a more spiritual way. Often you may feel that you have insights that come to provide solutions to your problems. The placement may indicate editorial activity or studies in metaphysical or religious subjects. It may also indicate artistic studies. Travel may also be for spiritual expansion, and you may also love long journeys...over the seas and far away.

11th: You express great sympathy and understanding to your friends and are generally generous often without boundaries towards them. You may share some artistic activities with your friends, and you may also have some shared metaphysical interests. Friends may have Pisces, Neptune, or Jupiter traits in their character. Beware of the people you choose to befriend as friends can become a source of deception or general disillusionment.

12th: You have unconscious spiritual wisdom which does not show on the surface. You have great empathy for humanity but often tend to isolate yourself and may also have feelings of loneliness. Your self-undoing may stem from an unconscious feeling of fogginess as well as a tendency to victimization and complain. Your hidden strength is your compassion.

a Available on Amazon

The Act of Manifestation: Tarot Techniques

Catherine S. Buck

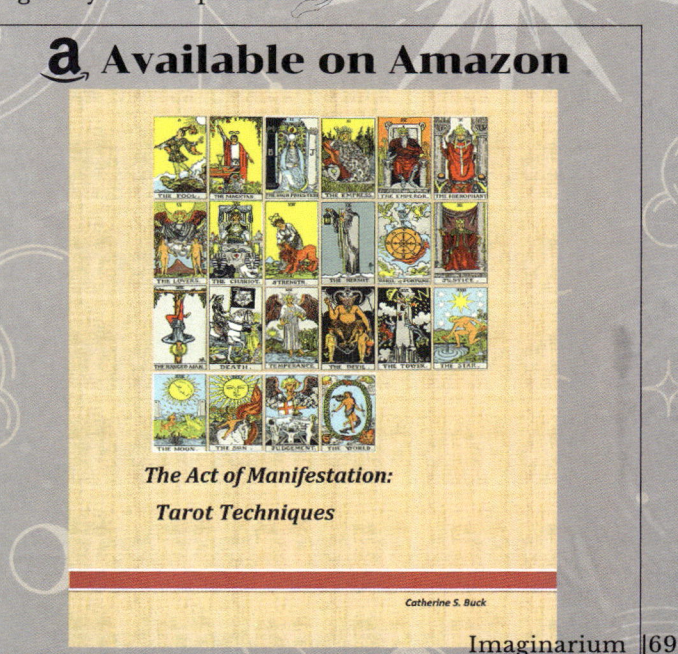

Imaginarium | 69

Astrology

Carl Jung & Astrology

By Yiannis Kokkinos

"Whatever is born or done at this particular moment of time has the quality of this moment of time." C.G.J.

Carl Gustav Jung was a pioneering Swiss psychologist known for his studies on the concepts of the theory of the Collective Consciousness, Synchronicity, Archetypes, etc. What he is less well known for is his astrological contribution to the field of psychology, and his use of astrology as a serious tool for exploring the depths of the human psyche. Jung was a contemporary and for a time a student of another great thinker, Sigmund Freud, upon whose psychoanalysis he built and developed his own analytical psychology. Of course, the link between astrology and psychology was - and is - something unthinkable in the scientific world and this cost him much of his life and reputation as he was trying to argue his ideas not only to his colleagues but also to himself. Fortunately for us, however, there have been great astrologers such as Stephen Arroyo, Dane Rudhyar, Liz Greene, Howard Sasportas, Karen Hamaker Zondag, Glenn Perry, Bruno & Louise Huber, etc. They took his thoughts and developed a new discipline, psychological and humanistic astrology, which is human-centred rather than event-oriented as it had been since the ancient times.

The reference to his extremely interesting work is long enough to be made here. He regarded astrology as the sum of all the psychological knowledge of antiquity. He had studied ancient Greek philosophers like Aristotle, Plato, Heraclitus, Pythagoras, and more modern ones like Schopenhauer, Kant, etc. Based on

Empedocles' thought that the Universe consists of four fundamental elements, Water, Air, Earth, and Fire; he defined four primordial images or main archetypes of human nature and behaviour: the Self, the Persona or Mask, the union of Anima and Animus or the Divine Couple, and the Shadow. He later found that these elements can be combined together to give a larger group of 12 archetypal images or archetypal figures into which human characters can be more clearly classified. At this point, it should be noted that the very popular Myers & Briggs personality test (Myers - Briggs Type Indicator, MBTI) is based on the same basis, but describes 16 types. Obviously, Jung chose the number twelve so that there would be a correspondence with the astrological signs of the zodiac. It is not known if he formally made any kind of connection, but we can identify the basic elements of each Jungian personality and link them to the character of the zodiac signs.

Aries: The Hero

Motto: Where there's a will, there's a way
Core desire: to prove one's worth through courageous acts
Goal: expert mastery in a way that improves the world
Greatest fear: weakness, vulnerability, being a "chicken"
Strategy: to be as strong and competent as possible
Weakness: arrogance, always needing another battle to fight
Talent: competence and courage

The Hero is also known as: The warrior, crusader, rescuer, superhero, the soldier, dragon slayer, the winner and the team leader.

Taurus: The Innocent

Motto: Free to be you and me
Core desire: to get to paradise
Goal: to be happy
Greatest fear: to be punished for doing something bad or wrong
Strategy: to do things right
Weakness: boring for all their naïve innocence
Talent: faith and optimism

The Innocent is also known as: Utopian, traditionalist, naïve, mystic, saint, romantic, dreamer.

Gemini: The Jester

Motto: You only live once
Core desire: to live in the moment with full enjoyment
Goal: to have a great time and lighten up the world
Greatest fear: being bored or boring others
Strategy: play, make jokes, be funny
Weakness: frivolity, wasting time
Talent: joy

The Jester is also known as: The fool, trickster, joker, practical joker or comedian.

Cancer: The Caregiver

Motto: Love your neighbour as yourself
Core desire: to protect and care for others
Goal: to help others
Greatest fear: selfishness and ingratitude
Strategy: doing things for others
Weakness: martyrdom and being exploited
Talent: compassion, generosity

The Caregiver is also known as: The saint, altruist, humane, parent, helper, supporter.

Leo - The Ruler

Motto: Power isn't everything; it's the only thing.
Core desire: control
Goal: create a prosperous, successful family or community
Strategy: exercise power
Greatest fear: chaos, being overthrown
Weakness: being authoritarian, unable to delegate
Talent: responsibility, leadership

The Ruler is also known as: The boss, leader, aristocrat, king, queen, politician, role model, manager or administrator.

Virgo: The Sage

Motto: The truth will set you free
Core desire: to find the truth.
Goal: to use intelligence and analysis to understand the world.
Biggest fear: being duped, misled—or ignorance.
Strategy: seeking out information and knowledge; self-reflection and understanding thought processes.
Weakness: can study details forever and never act.
Talent: wisdom, intelligence.

The Sage is also known as: The expert, scholar, detective, advisor, thinker, philosopher, academic, researcher, thinker, planner, professional, mentor, teacher, contemplative.

Carl G. Jung
1875 - 1961

Libra: The Lover

Motto: You're the only one
Core desire: intimacy and experience
Goal: being in a relationship with the people, work and surroundings they love
Greatest fear: being alone, a wallflower, unwanted, unloved
Strategy: to become more and more physically and emotionally attractive
Weakness: outward-directed desire to please others at risk of losing own identity
Talent: passion, gratitude, appreciation, and commitment

The Lover is also known as: The partner, friend, intimate, enthusiast, sensualist, spouse, team-builder.

Scorpio - The Magician

Motto: I make things happen.
Core desire: understanding the fundamental laws of the universe
Goal: to make dreams come true
Greatest fear: unintended negative consequences
Strategy: develop a vision and live by it
Weakness: becoming manipulative
Talent: finding win-win solutions

The Magician is also known as: The visionary, catalyst, originator, charismatic leader, shaman, healer, medicine man.

Sagittarius: The Explorer

Motto: Don't fence me in
Core desire: the freedom to find out who you are through exploring the world
Goal: to experience a better, more authentic, more fulfilling life
Biggest fear: getting trapped, conformity, inner emptiness
Strategy: journey, seeking out and experiencing new things, escape from boredom
Weakness: aimless wandering, becoming a misfit
Talent: autonomy, ambition, being true to one's soul

The explorer is also known as: The seeker, iconoclast, wanderer, individualist, pilgrim.

Imaginarium |72

Capricorn: The Everyman

Motto: All men and women are created equal
Core Desire: connecting with others
Goal: to belong
Greatest fear: to be left out or to stand out from the crowd
Strategy: develop ordinary solid virtues, be down to earth, the common touch
Weakness: losing one's own self in an effort to blend in or for the sake of superficial relationships
Talent: realism, comprehension, lack of pretence

The Everyman is also known as: The good old boy, regular guy/girl, the person next door, the realist, the working stiff, the solid citizen, the good neighbour, the silent majority.

Aquarius: The Rebel

Motto: Rules are made to be broken
Core desire: revenge or revolution
Goal: to overturn what isn't working
Greatest fear: to be powerless or ineffectual
Strategy: disrupt, destroy, or shock
Weakness: crossing over to the dark side, crime
Talent: outrageousness, radical freedom

The Outlaw is also known as: The rebel, revolutionary, wild man, the misfit, or iconoclast.

Pisces: The Creator/Artist

Motto: If you can imagine it, it can be done
Core desire: to create things of enduring value
Goal: to realize a vision
Greatest fear: mediocre vision or execution
Strategy: develop artistic control and skill
Task: to create culture, express own vision
Weakness: perfectionism, bad solutions
Talent: creativity and imagination

The Creator is also known as: The artist, inventor, innovator, reformer, musician, writer or dreamer.

Carl Jung's Red Book, his own private diary, is full of astrological notes and extraordinary illustrations.

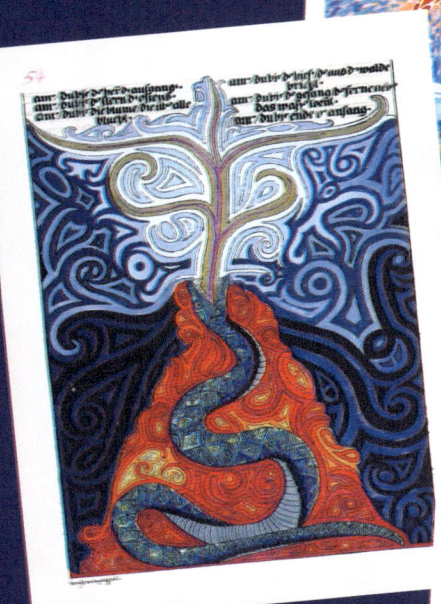

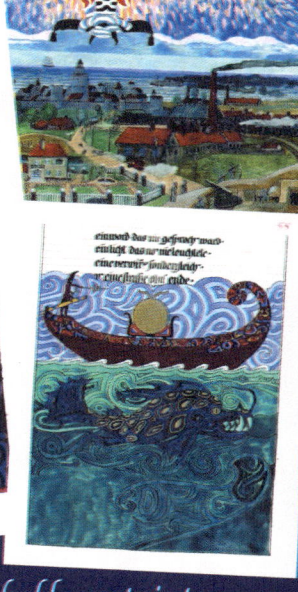

"One can expect, with remarkable certainty, that a precisely defined psychological state will be accompanied by the corresponding astrological configuration." C.G.J.

We may not recognize ourselves in some of these descriptions or they may not agree perfectly with what we know now, but let us not forget three things. Firstly, we are not just our Sun - while sometimes our Sun sign is not the most obvious. We are all mixtures of astrological and psychological archetypes in varying proportions, which even change over time. Secondly, Jung was NOT an astrologer. His second daughter, Gret Baumann-Jung, became an astrologer so she could help her father with the charts of the people he studied. And thirdly he was the founder of psychological astrology in modern times so he had no information from anywhere else to draw on. That is, he was a pioneer who, even if he made mistakes, his work and thoughts remain admired as do his contributions, which as we noted he paid with a high price - with personal humiliation and rejections. All of which, as it happens today, came from people not knowledgeable in astrology or knowledgeable only in "astrology the TV and magazine columns".

Quotes: https://astroligion.com/20-carl-jung-quotes-on-astrology/
Photos by Yiannis Kokkinos

THE DICTATORSHIP OF GOOD INTENTIONS

Aquarius

By Yiannis Kokkinos

Aquarius, with Uranus as its ruler, as we all know, is, among other things, the sign of rebellion (uprising) per se. Essentially, however, it is called Revolution which means revolving. To be more precise: Aquarius is the sign that wants to bring the ups down and the downs up. The forcible overthrow, the "turning of the wheel". In astrology, this is in the eleventh (11th) house.

For those who do not know, the astrological chart is circular, divided into twelve sections, and has a clear sequence in its structure. Starting from the first section and reaching the last one, the twelfth, we pass through different "areas" which symbolize specific stages of development areas and needs of man. Each step (corresponding to a house and a sign) in the chart represents some necessary lessons to be learned before successfully moving on to the next. For example, we cannot become good parents in the 4th house or Cancer unless we first learn to think and communicate properly in the 3rd house or Gemini; we cannot communicate with others unless we first come into close contact with the material environment around us through the 2nd house or Taurus, and so on.

Let us now look at Aquarius and its corresponding eleventh house. The proper/good cause of a revolution is to overthrow an evil establishment in order to bring progress to society and humanity. That is, to overthrow any tyrannical government, any inhuman regime that oppresses its citizens, in order to establish a peaceful democratic, and just state that respects and counts everyone equally. But this means that BEFORE the overthrow takes place before the revolution even manifests itself, the successor state must be ready and functional: the government of the new regime to which we want to transfer power. Otherwise, if we "overthrow" one government without putting another in its place, mob rule, lawlessness, destruction, and dissolution will soon follow.

The natural progression of the 11th house is the 12th, Pisces. In the twelfth house, humanity is called upon to experience the ultimate ideal: spiritual understanding, unfeigned love, total union, the highest and most perfect level of evolution to which all souls, all consciousnesses, can reach and harmoniously connect as one, without the need to impose by force on anyone. Each person will know and understand his or her particular role within the greater whole, respecting and fulfilling justly his or her obligations to others. It sounds too good to be true, and the course of humanity to date confirms it. Besides, if a single individual in millions wants to violate this condition, the whole fish structure collapses.

> Healthy Aquarian rebelliousness is necessary to drive a healthy society to the highest levels of coexistence. But even if Aquarius can function healthily, society is still not ready – at least for now.

In practice, at least at present, societies need laws and limits to function. This means that any new governance brought by the Aquarian revolutions, even if it has indeed come with the best of intentions, necessarily imposes restrictions and rules on those who would want to oppose it or not behave beneficially, in order for it to continue to exist. So, without judging here whether it is right or wrong (1), it will still oppress a part of society. And as this portion grows, or as more and more dissatisfied groups appear who oppose the new government and what it stands for, the more intense the repression that our revolution is "forced" to exercise.
So what do we see? That yes, healthy Aquarian rebelliousness is necessary to drive a healthy society to the highest levels of coexistence. But even if Aquarius can function healthily, society is still not ready - at least for now. As a result, instead of evolving naturally from the 11th house by moving on to the next, the 12th, we are essentially back to the conservative 10th house! In other words, the progressive government is gradually losing its vision and character and is being transformed into the very thing that it overthrew. In order for a new revolution to be born and the cycle to repeat itself.

In political (mundane) astrology negative characteristics of the 12th house are the secret enemies of the state "within" and "outside" the borders, surveillance, spies and espionage, murders, prisons, reformatories, crime wherever it comes from, secret organizations and cartels, - in general everything dark and illegal concerning every level and structure of the country. Also are the charity benefits (grants) to the weaker classes, hospitals, and the collapse of the economy. If we think about it, all of this is also about a vicious transition from the 11th to the 12th through a revolution that did not find the right conditions, the right ground to come to fruition. As a result, we are led back into a difficult 10th again waiting for the repeat of the project. So is the Aquarian change futile? As long as it teaches us at least something, as long as we as a whole as humans take even a small step forward, no.

(1): Right and wrong like good and evil are concepts that are usually shaped by our logic, morality, and personal way of dealing with things. Let's look at a simplistic example: a fly finds itself trapped in a spider web. Exactly the same event for the fly is "bad" because it means death, while for the spider it is "good" because it means that it will be fed and live. We, looking at it as external observers, would consider it unimportant since it is simply nature doing its job. But if for whatever reason we connected with one of the two animals, either consciously or unconsciously, the outcome would affect us personally and we would take a stand and therefore judge it and even subjectively.

Good and evil have been of concern to man from antiquity (Plato, Aristotle) to modern philosophy and theology. Countless thoughts and opinions, some of them controversial, have been expressed. Many tyrannical regimes and countless crimes have been based on distorted interpretations of this dipole. But the fact remains that evil exists, and as Plato says, it functions as the opposite concept of good in order to achieve order, balance, and harmony. Without the existence of evil, the concept of education aimed at preventing it and pursuing good might not be considered important. And by education (paedea in Greek) we mean not only formal academic education but our lifelong evolutionary journey in how to become more fulfilled human beings.

Imaginarium |75

Divination

Victorian Floramancy

by Marcia Gascoyne-Masino
Author of Best Tarot Practices & Easy Tarot Guide

Floramancy was the Victorian obsession with flower omens and prophecy. They believed that flowers emanated specific energy messages and because they were and are sensitive, they could also respond to hostile or positive influences. A specific flower could communicate love code on your behalf, warn you of impending danger and even predict your future.

Flower meanings have ancient folklore roots when they were believed to be sacred representations of the Greek and Roman gods and goddesses. Violets were the blood of the ancestors coming up from the ground. Myrtle was the sweetness of love delivered by the angels. The Victorians adopted then adapted the old-world meanings and reinvented them to reflect their fascination with romance. Nosegays, small floral corsages with specific flowers that had secret love meanings became popular. When worn over the heart the flower messaged "I love you" if on the lapel it signalled "friends only."

The Victorians also changed the concept of childhood, because it was viewed as separate from adulthood by the growing middle class for the first time. Children were to be kept innocent and dependent on their parents and they could read! Queen Victoria herself mandated education for all and not just for learning. This era brought children's books like Alice in Wonderland and Treasure Island into the new childhood experience and reading was for pleasure.

Floramancy inevitably found its way into Victorian children's literature. Often associated to the Spring, the symbolic time of childhood, one example describes flower fairies dancing around a small child named Aurora on a warm moonlit night. "It was a "pink night" and fairies doing as the "fine" people do for their dinner parties they kept to one color." In Victorian times pink roses signified innocent love, affection, grace, gentleness, joy and happiness.

From the 1887 story, The Fairy "Content" by Jessie Benton Fremont, "There was a strange great rosy light over half the sky and the fairies were gliding about and looking up and wondering at the strange sight. At first the light was a lovely watermelon pink with cool green and white lights shooting up through the pink into the middle of the sky. The light settled into a wide band of strong white light spanning the entire horizon in a firmament of deep blue."

"This lasted more than an hour. It happened

that was the first hour of the life of a little girl named Aurora. The splendid brilliance of the midnight sky was taken as a good omen and the wise Orientals would've made a fine horoscope for this little one." (Her horoscope would've had a dawn ascendant timing, possibly an Aries, Taurus or Gemini Spring birthday with the same sign as the ascendant.) "Certainly, some of the good fairies stood by that cradle and made their gifts of that one can be sure."

Fremont's story features floramancy because each flower had a character trait to give to Aurora as a gift. "The Rose and Lily are queens of beauty and they can give that; the tulips with their golden raiment represent wealth and love of show; the Camelia so perfect in form but without fragrance, gives cold selfishness and pride. The sweet pink hyacinth gave its own sweetness and rose and lily gave the baby girl her coloring and a little purple violet gave her modesty and the gift of just giving pleasure by their presence. But the crowning gift came from the plain little pink clover, the fairy content. The fairy said, "I cannot give you beauty or riches but I give you content."

Folklore about Spring flowers include predictive meanings. Watch for the first flower you see in springtime because the initial of that flower's name will belong to someone important to you in the upcoming year. There's an old Welsh legend that if you're the first to spot the early daffodils of the season, you'll be rewarded by a year of good luck and gold. A popular spring flower, Daffodil is associated with joy and rebirth but folklore decries never give one for fear of bad luck, only give a bunch.

Victorian Flower meanings

Peony - because the ant has to labor to open the bud the flower represented reward for industriousness especially romantic. The peony was the flower a man gave his lady love once he had successfully courted her. It ended up in many Victorian bridal bouquets with a combined symbolic message of bashfulness, shame and purity. Love and fruition are a standard peony theme along with good fortune, peace, prosperity, happy home, healing and marriage.

Also known as the Chinese peony or "the queen of flowers" (common garden peony) it represents optimism, nobility, fame (it was once the national flower of China) and wealth. Japan regards them as the "king of flowers" they are courage and honor. A full peony bush is lucky, however watch out for faded or discolored flowers or dried leaves said to portent disaster. An odd number of blooms is also considered bad luck.

Geraniums – The Victorians must have had held geraniums in high regard because they mention many types each with specific positive or negative qualities attributed to them. The Lemon Geranium meant an unexpected meeting, nutmeg an expected meeting. The ivy geranium was necessary for a bridal bouquet because it symbolized favor. Dark ones were melancholy, scarlet was comforting, silver leaved meant recall, oak leaved true friendship, rose scented was preference and horseshoe leafed was stupidity!

Generally, geraniums are good wishes and friendship. White ones for fertility, pink for romance and red ones for protection since when placed near your doorway they will turn to face the direction of an approaching stranger acting as a horticultural home security system.

Day Lilies - Coquetry because it blooms in the day and withers in the evening, so doesn't stay around long. It's a flower with a reputation for flirty romantic advances, dalliances and trifling with affections. Don't worry, the hurt of being seduced will soon be forgotten because day lily denotes forgetfulness which comes in handy when you want to get over a loss or to give to someone when you want to say fuhgeddaboudit. Red and dark orange ones are really passionate and the standard orange and yellow ones are joyful beauty. White is always purity and pink romantic. In contrast, the older traditional meaning is motherhood and in Chinese folklore if a pregnant woman wears a day lily, she will give birth to a boy.

Coneflowers – Purple Echinacea represents strength because they are hearty and long lasting. A North American flower, from the perspective of indigenous beliefs it is one of the sacred life medicine healing flowers. Coneflower has also been chewed ritually during sweat lodge ceremonies and the Sundance. Often used in spell casting to enhance its power. This flower if carried on your person is believed to keep your spirit strong during challenging times.

For the Victorians the Sunflower had happy traits of warmth and energy and it was considered good luck to receive one when starting afresh. Most likely the analogy between sunrise and the dawn of a new day and the sun shaped flower was the reasoning behind the fresh start meaning. The Chinese consider it a symbol of longevity and it was consumed by the royal family to enhance their lifespan.

Rose – generally red is deep passionate love, yellow friendship, white spirituality and pink ones represent femininity, elegance, refinement and sweetness; a warm darker pink is a thank you rose symbolizing gratitude and recognition.

Today florists use design themes such as flowers of the month and astrological signs, after all flowers and birthdays go together. It's considered lucky to wear your zodiac flower.

Aries – Red roses and tulips, honeysuckle

Taurus - Poppy, rose lavender, lilac, lily of the valley and sweet pea

Gemini - foxglove. Lily of the valley, lavender, daffodil

Cancer – white flowers especially roses, iris, cornflower, delphinium

Leo – marigold, gerbera dahlia, sunflower

Virgo - buttercup, small flowers, wild flowers, violet

Libra- bluebell, gardenia, tea roses, freesia, gladiola

Scorpio - peony, anthurium, chrysanthemum

Sagittarius - carnation, crocus, blazing star

Capricorn – pansy, jasmine, violet

Aquarius - orchid, lily, pitcher plant

Pisces – water lily, narcissus, jasmine, lilac

It's hard to find a contemporary example of floramancy. However, Kate Middleton was inspired by Victorian flower symbolism when designing her wedding bouquet. When she married Prince William she chose flowers that had relationship and romantic meanings. Myrtle and ivy for love, fidelity and marriage; hyacinth for sports (they are said to have a bond over a shared love of athletics) and sweet william for bravery (a reference to William). She could've added flowers for their zodiac signs too, Capricorn jasmine for her and white roses for William with his sun in Cancer and their shared Moon in Cancer.

The Victorians did create elaborate bouquets based on floramancy called florigraphy; the imagination reels at the possible combinations with secret messages from the giver to the recipient.

Excerpt from The Fairy "Content" by Jessie Benton Fremont was published in Wide Awake Story Book for Our Boys and Girls, Lothrop Publishing Company, 1897.

Marcia began her metaphysical career early. She co-owned a tea room, bookstore and had a daily radio talk show featuring the occult, new age and astrology. Because she encountered many clients and listeners from all walks of life seeking guidance, she developed an easy-to-understand metaphysical vernacular for her tarot and astrology readings including a blend of astrology and tarot interpretation designed to help and guide each person. Marcia wrote two best seller books on the Tarot, Easy Tarot Guide and Best Tarot Practices, both available on Amazon and through your local bookseller. She is the creator of two limited edition Tarot Decks - The Spirit Light Tarot and The Fountain of Light Tarot as well as The Lily Dale Oracle cards inspired by Spiritualism. Her current projects include The New Spirit Light Tarot Deck and she has branched out into mainstream writing with a metaphysical twist.

Contact marciamasinoastrotarotart@yahooo.com
https://mmasino.wixsite.com/tarotbooks

Imaginarium |79

Tarot

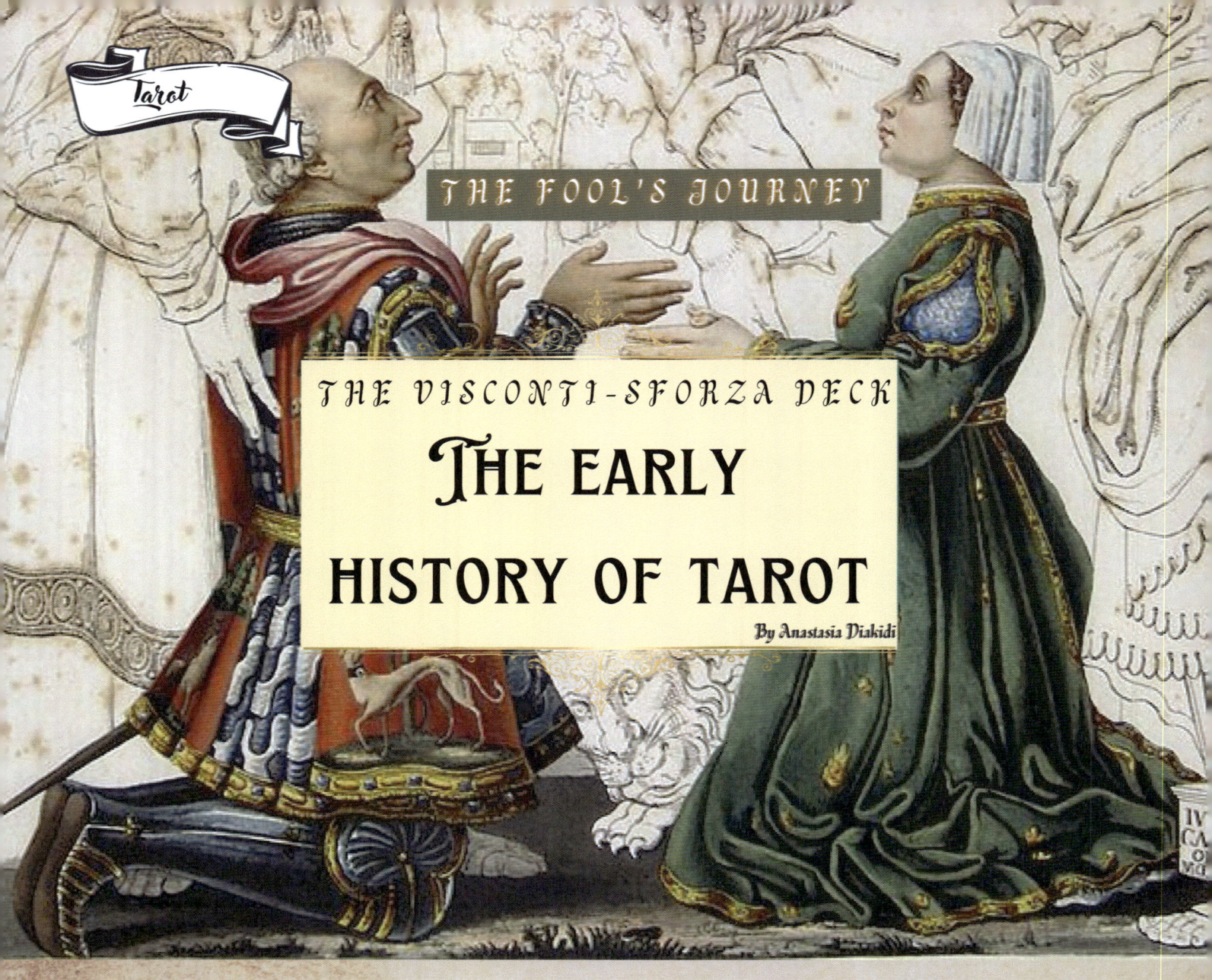

THE FOOL'S JOURNEY

THE VISCONTI-SFORZA DECK
The Early History of Tarot

By Anastasia Diakidi

The origins of the tarot have a long and in many ways dubious history. However, the original use of the deck is confirmed by historians that it was created not as a means of divination but as a deck of playing cards.

Between the 15th and 18th centuries, the tarot was used as a card game and decks were commissioned by great Italian noble families. The first known reference to a tarot deck comes from Ferrara, Italy, circa 1442.

Later, decks of cards became popular among the public and began to be used in taverns as a gambling game with rules similar to those of today's bridge. Most of these decks unfortunately do not survive as they were made with very cheap and flimsy materials.

In Italy, France, and Spain the game of tarot continued to be played until the 20th century even when tarot became a divination tool.

The Visconti-Sforza deck is the earliest deck available. It is almost complete and there are cards that are missing. The deck is now in Bergamo, Italy, and in New York. Four of the cards-those of the Tower, the Devil, the 3 of Swords as well as the Knight of Pentacles-are missing.

Historians believe that the deck was created by Francesco Sforza who was a military commander who married the wealthy Bianca Maria Visconti, the daughter of Philip Maria Visconti, the Duke of Milan. The deck of cards was created as a gift to celebrate the marriage and the union of the two families.

The story goes that Sforza was pursuing power and wanted to become Duke of Milan in place of his father-in-law. When that didn't happen, he with the help and support of his wife used his military power and claimed Milan as his own. A strategy that eventually delivered the dukedom to him.

The deck of cards is full of the symbols of the two families. For example, in the Emperor and Empress card, we see the laurel and palm leaves, symbols of the Visconti, while the three connected rings are symbols of the Sforza.

Top Left: The Star
Right: The Magician
Bottom: The Popess

Imaginarium | 81

symbols of the deck, named it the Visconti tarot.

Later Count Colleoni offered 26 cards to his friend Count Francesco Ballioni. When Ballioni died in 1901, he left all his cards at the Academia Carrara in Bergamo. The 15 cards found in the Morgan Library and Museum in New York were donated by the Colleoni family in 1911, but the family still has 13 cards in their collection to this day.

The Major Arcana of the deck has no numbers and as mentioned above the Tower and the Devil are missing. It is not known if these cards as well as the other two missing cards of the Minor Arcana were originally in the deck and were lost or if they were simply never created. Now that the deck has been recreated, the missing cards have been designed with influences from 15th-century Italian artistic traditions of other decks.

The deck of cards is the work of the artist Bonifacio Bembo. He hand-painted all the cards except for six cards of the Major Arcana which were painted by another artist. These cards are the Sun, Moon, World, Star, Fortitude, and Temperance. All the cards have the symbols of the families, as previously mentioned, as well as other geometric shapes. The original deck was produced around 1450 and may also be associated with the School of Francesco Zavatari.

The example of the Visconti-Forza was followed by other families where they created their own tarot decks with their own symbols from region to region. These decks created mainly in Milan, Bologna, and Ferrara by the end of the 15th century are works of real artistry; they are hand-painted with tempera and gold-plated on sturdy card stock.

Today, the deck of cards has been recreated and is available in the market. The interpretations of the modern deck have been worked out based on the original interpretations where they clearly had Christian concepts in both the interpretative approach and the illustrations. Today the cards are considered by many scholars to be archetypal. That is, they represent Tarot archetypes in their purest expression.

The 74 cards of the original Visconti-Sforza deck are now in three museums: 26 cards are in the Academia Carrara in Bergamo, Italy; 35 cards are in the Morgan Library and Museum in New York; and 13 cards are in a private collection belonging to the Colleoni family, also in Bergamo.

There is no record of the cards in the archives of the Visconti-Sforza families, probably due to the multiple destructions of Milan over the centuries. In the 17th century, however, we have the first evidence of the deck when Count Abiviani gave the cards to the Donati family. They in turn sold them to Colleoni at the end of the 19th century who, after an analysis of the

Many cards contain either heraldic motifs, aristocratic, militaristic attire or inscriptions such as "a bon droyt" or "amor myo".

Book your astrological consultations online

- Natal Chart analysis
- Synastry analysis
- Horary analysis

https://imaginariumworld.co.uk/book-online

The Wands

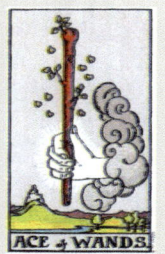

The wands are associated with the element of fire, the masculine principle, and their phallic shape represents dynamic and creative energy. They often appear in business matters and those involving initiatives and energetic beginnings.

ACE

The beginning of an activity or the origin of a situation. The birth or a new beginning. The card has fertile energy and indicates success in social, financial and artistic matters. It can be seen to be associated with ancestors and inheritance. It also symbolizes action, passion, and will in both a project and a sexual relationship. With Ace, we are called upon to take an assertive place in things and use our strength and assertiveness.

We are called to express ourselves creatively and also to believe in ourselves. It motivates us to move forward in a healthy yet joyful way. In a professional matter it can also mean a hiring or a promotion, while in a love matter, it can represent a man with a strong libido or the beginning of a sexual relationship. In love matters, it also points us to have initiative as well as passion.

If you are facing obstacles in your life, the Ace suggests that you should face events forcefully, to learn the right way to move forward and also to act based on ideas you are inspired by.

TWO

Power, influence on others, good luck, and wealth. The card symbolizes cooperation, partnership, and teamwork.

The card motivates us to make decisions based on our intuition but also to create something new and innovative that will help us find our place in the world. It tells us that we can convince others of our abilities but also leave our mark on the world. It is a card that speaks to both inventiveness and diversity. It is important to welcome new ideas to broaden our perspectives but also to move forward with confidence and faith.

In a professional matter, it may represent business, travel or financial support. It is also possible that it may indicate a marriage or affair that improves finances. The card is positive and is particularly favourable for business affairs. Two calls us to examine responsibilities and evaluate the care and attention we give to what is under our control.

Imaginarium |84

THREE

Exploration, travel, trade, and discovery. The card speaks to success in business, arts, and commerce, especially in everything connected with the sea, creative arts, and freelancing. Generosity and hopes that are realized. Collaborative spirit and partnerships that establish the enterprise. The card also indicates foresight as well as expansion. It invites us to see the bigger picture but also to prepare for the future and what is to come. We may need to consider new information or find a clever way to act. It states that knowledge has power and by realizing our intentions we will find our mission. The card may indicate that we are seeking new adventures or generally have an open mind to a new journey, either literal or metaphorical.

In a business matter, it may indicate successful endeavours, good product that brings profits, and also expansion into foreign markets.

In an emotional matter, the card indicates a good marriage, and can also mean that physical appearance can make an impression. Of course, it speaks of relationships looking ahead to the future.

FOUR

The successful completion of an activity, a consolidated situation, consolidation of profits. Peace, quiet and rest after an achievement. Joyful family life, retreat and country life.
The card speaks of solid foundations but also a strong community. It can symbolize land but also property and can appear when we want to expand our domestic situation. The card speaks of favours, celebrations and public relations.

It motivates us to enjoy domestic harmony, to be proud of our accomplishments and also to free ourselves from expectations coming from other people or other emotional burdens. It is a card that shows us a pleasant event, motivates to cherish and enjoy life. It is a celebration of freedom. The time when we rejoice in the outcome of our labours.

In a business matter, it can speak of providing services, benefits from hospitality or entertainment, real estate investment, buying a house and other gains or investments.

In an love reading, it may indicate a communicative relationship as well as cohabitation, marriage and mutual support.

FIVE

Battle for success. Also arguments, struggles and ordeals. Sports. Fair play, constructive feedback, enjoyable debate, competition, test of power. Cooperation is the key.

On this card, we will have to fight to succeed. It can show us obstacles that force us to resort to competition. It can show quarrels and also irritating reactions to collaborations with others. It is possible that we may be annoyed with the opinions of others or there may be frustrating circumstances. The card may also show an unsuccessful attempt to defend ourselves against a forceful competitor. It is a challenge card and you may feel like you don't know where to stand.

In a business matter, it can represent a strong competitor, problems between employers and employees and the struggle for dominance in the market.

In a love issue, it can indicate the competitive relationship, quarrels and the possibility that the querent may be under love siege by more than one person!

SIX

Hard work brings rewards. Victory. Confidence and great success. Admiration, recognition, and popularity.
The card shows how our actions are applauded and through them, we feel fulfilled. We may be the centre of attention. Some news is coming about a victory. Pride and superiority, however, the card warns us not to be too proud and not to become arrogant.

In a professional matter, it can show the profits, the funding, and also a marketing campaign to make a mark in the market. It can also show a star or a professional athlete.

In a love issue, the cards indicates that we can win over the person we are interested in and suggests that we should be confident.

SEVEN

A challenge can be overcome with courage and strength. Threat. Battle. The need to rely on and defend ourselves.
The card speaks of a battle we must fight to defend our beliefs, our acquisitions and our principles. It tells us to stand firmly on our ground and remain unmoved by anything that threatens our principles and our position.

The card indicates a defensive attitude. We are called to take a fighting stance but also to say no to others, to set boundaries with determination.

The card tells us to show strength against our opponents but it is very important to know what we are fighting a battle for as it can also indicate a meaningless battle.

In a business or financial matter, it can indicate a fight for finances or the need to protect finances from overspending or losses.

In a love reading, it can indicate the need to protect our relationship.

Imaginarium |85

Photo Canva Stock

EIGHT

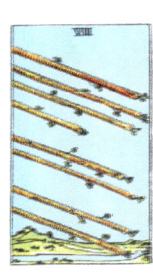

Speed, fast-moving developments, issues coming to a quick close, urgent messages, haste. The arrows of love.
After the fierce resistance you had to put up in the seventh card, now help comes quickly. It shows hope that something is rapidly coming to an end.
The card also shows us taking quick action, receiving an important message, or generally discovering what was missing and reassessing our decisions. It may urge us to sort out our priorities or clarify our intentions. In any case, developments are fast even if everything is up in the air, they will soon come to a positive conclusion.

In a business matter, it may indicate repayment. It may show that we are taking on a lot because we have long-term plans.

In an emotional issue, it can indicate an acquaintance or a long-distance relationship and generally a love affair that is progressing at a very fast pace.

NINE

Enduring strength, resistance, courage. Never-give-up attitude. Perseverance brings rewards and gains. Also, delay.
With this card, we find the courage and strength to continue. We may need to learn something about ourselves that we didn't know or find out exactly what we believe and through that discovery realize that we are stronger than we thought.

The card speaks of defending oneself and the family. It urges us to be patient and persistent and favours strength through self-awareness. Another indication is suspicion towards others, there may be guardedness or feeling vulnerable resulting in being ready for anything and worrying about the future. This may also be based on past hurts that come back to us and cause us to worry about the future.

In a professional matter, it can indicate increased obligations, strict hours, supervision as well as high demands or standards. Generally, there can be pressure in business yet achievement. Perhaps a time of austerity that requires caution in spending.

In an emotional matter, it may show jealousy in the relationship and also the need to look objectively at the future of the relationship.

TEN

A heavy burden to carry, excessive demands, martyrdom. The final test of willpower. The completion of what began with the Ace. Caution as achievements can become burdens or failures. Important not to be unfair or pressurise ourselves out of an excessive eagerness to please others. The card may indicate too many responsibilities that bring physical pain, such as backache and a blockage of thought.
It may also indicate a sense of responsibility or even guilt as a price to be paid. The card may also indicate only work and no fun.

In a professional matter, it will show excessive demands and also workaholism.

In an emotional issue, it shows that the relationship is creating a burden or that one partner has been shouldering all the responsibilities.

PAGE

Passion and determination. An attention seeker. Fiery personality; quick, energetic and daring. A risk taker. A reliable messenger, a trustworthy person.
Whether as a person or as a situation, the card symbolizes new ideas, confidence, insight, and enthusiasm.
It may indicate other individuals or it may indicate that you are a childlike or exuberant person, and you are not lacking in creativity and enthusiasm in the venture you have taken up. It indicates that you may be willing to go in a new direction, take an opportunity, and move forward with light-hearted creativity.
The card reminds us to have faith in ourselves.
Like all Pages, it speaks of messages of all kinds. With this card, you may receive some news.

On a professional issue, it speaks of work-related travel, changing direction in a profession, or taking on a job you've never done before.

In a love issue, it may indicate good news from the person you are interested in and generally good communication between the two. It can also indicate the risk you need to take with childlike enthusiasm to take the relationship in a new direction and also to enjoy good times in it.

KNIGHT

The card may indicate a young person who is generally charming, passionate, and hot-tempered. He may also be very self-confident and lovable. Generally generous and friendly but unpredictable.
As a situation, the Knight may indicate a change of residence, flight, separation, or departure. It indicates the creative force that pushes us forward to realize our plans. Once these are realized we move on to the next project.

It can also indicate that you are a confident person, perhaps a little vain, charming but often lacking in sensitivity, seductive but with more lust. It can also indicate that you want to be loved but don't want to belong anywhere as you are people who prefer to be on the journey rather than the destination. You are people of action and adventure with the gift of words.

Imaginarium |87

In a business matter, it can indicate competitive entry into the market, loans, credit purchases, or instalments.

In an emotional matter, it shows enthusiasm and passion but it may pass quickly.

QUEEN

An affectionate and charming woman. A stable character, practical and calm. A popular person quite authoritative and determined yet kind and generous. She is intolerant of opposition. Good friend and ally.

The Queen represents the emotional will. As a condition, it can indicate a friendship to come. It can also indicate a need for us to be supportive and give friendly advice to someone.

She advises us to follow our true passion, create harmony, and also to be goal-oriented and ambitious. It is also important to be independent, busy, and active. The card also indicates that we may remain undaunted in the face of a challenge or generally committed to a project.

It shows charismatic, creative people, women who know where they are going and are generally career-oriented, and people who are attractive, charming, and charismatic can belong to the sign of Leo and be sexually active.

In a professional matter, it speaks of hard work and goal achievement, while in an emotional matter, it may indicate intense sexuality and even pregnancy.

KING

Honesty, centred will, integrity.

As an individual, the King may speak of someone who has practical skills on a subject, is a boss, or is generally bossy by nature. He is usually a male authority figure who possesses talents and gifts. He has a vital and vibrant energy and is not lacking in increased activity and a touch of melodrama.

As a situation, it can speak to perfecting an art, grandiose plans, and the need to become an authority figure who inspires others by setting a good example. You may be willing to take risks as you have confidence in yourself as well as insight.

In a professional matter, you will see new and exciting projects, goal achievement, profits, proper and division of labour. It may show individuals good in technology and excellent entrepreneurial skills.

In a romantic issue, it may indicate a work acquaintance or even a relationship with a person who has the above characteristics and generally is protective, passionate, generous, and talented.

Photo Canva Stock

Ancient Wisdom

The Orphic Hymn to Helios

Hear golden Titan, whose eternal eye
with broad survey, illumines all the sky.
Self-born, unwearied in diffusing light,
and to all eyes the mirror of delight:
Lord of the seasons, with thy fiery car
and leaping coursers, beaming light from far:
With thy right hand the source of morning light,
and with thy left the father of the night.
Agile and vigorous, venerable Sun,
fiery and bright around the heavens you run.
Foe to the wicked, but the good man's guide,
o'er all his steps propitious you preside:
With various founding, golden lyre,
'tis mine to fill the world with harmony divine.
Father of ages, guide of prosperous deeds,
the world's commander, borne by lucid steeds,
Immortal Jove, all-searching, bearing light,
source of existence, pure and fiery bright
Bearer of fruit, almighty lord of years,
agile and warm, whom every power reveres.
Great eye of Nature and the starry skies,
doomed with immortal flames to set and rise
Dispensing justice, lover of the stream,
the world's great despot, and o'er all supreme.
Faithful defender, and the eye of right,
of steeds the ruler, and of life the light:
With founding whip four fiery steeds you guide,
when in the car of day you glorious ride.
Propitious on these mystic labors shine,
and bless thy suppliants with a life divine.

Translated by Thomas Taylor

The Orphic Hymn to Helios can be recited on Sundays, particularly around noon when the Sun is at the highest point. Recommended to burn frankincense or light a yellow/orange candle while chanting the hymn.

Gift Ideas by IMAGINARIUM
For Modern Witches!

Visit
www.imaginariumworld.co.uk

Beauty & Home Products

100% natural
Ethical
Eco

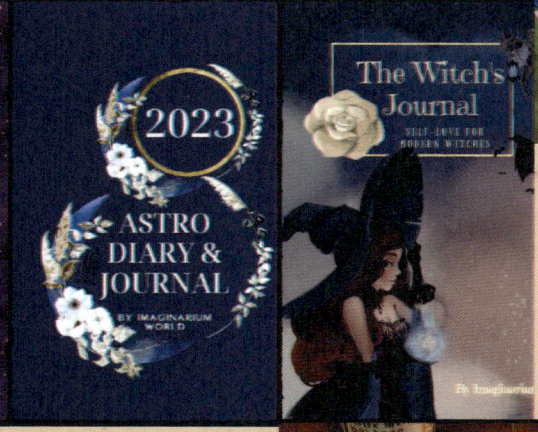

Notebooks - Journals - Planners

Your words have power to change your day, your life, the world!

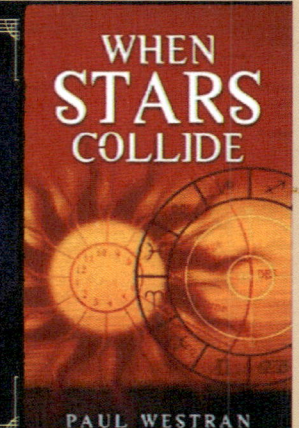

Books

Enchanting authors share their 'magic'!

BEAUTIFUL
TAROT DECKS

*Artistic
Insightful
Sophisticated*

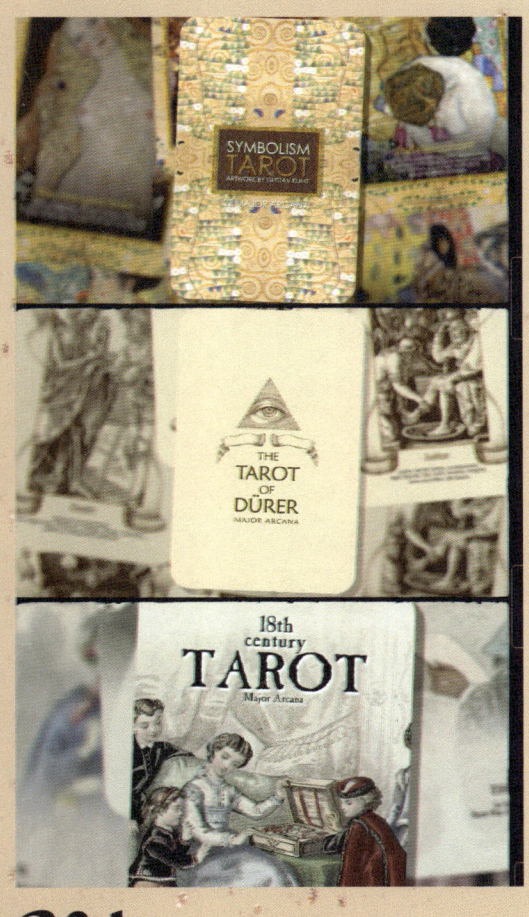

BY
IBIZA
TAROT

MADE WITH LOVE

Imaginarium 91

Printed in Great Britain
by Amazon